PALADINS TALE

Story & Art by Alexis E. Fajardo

Cover & Interior Colors by Jose Mari Flores

An untold tale from the pages of *The Song of Roland!*

When the Franks are ambushed by the Saracens deep in the Pyrenees mountains, King Charlemagne's elite knights, the Peers, are accused of high treason. Betrayed, framed, and locked away, the king's men escape to fight another day!

bonus story!

Lookin' For Lingonberries!

When 12-year-old Beowulf dreams of lingo... is go and look for some, but what he finds... Can Beowulf survive a day in the wild or w... become a Heathobard's b...

D1057695

Print ISBN 978-0-9909505-1-6
Kid Beowulf is © and ™ 2017 Alexis E. Fajardo – kidbeowulf.com

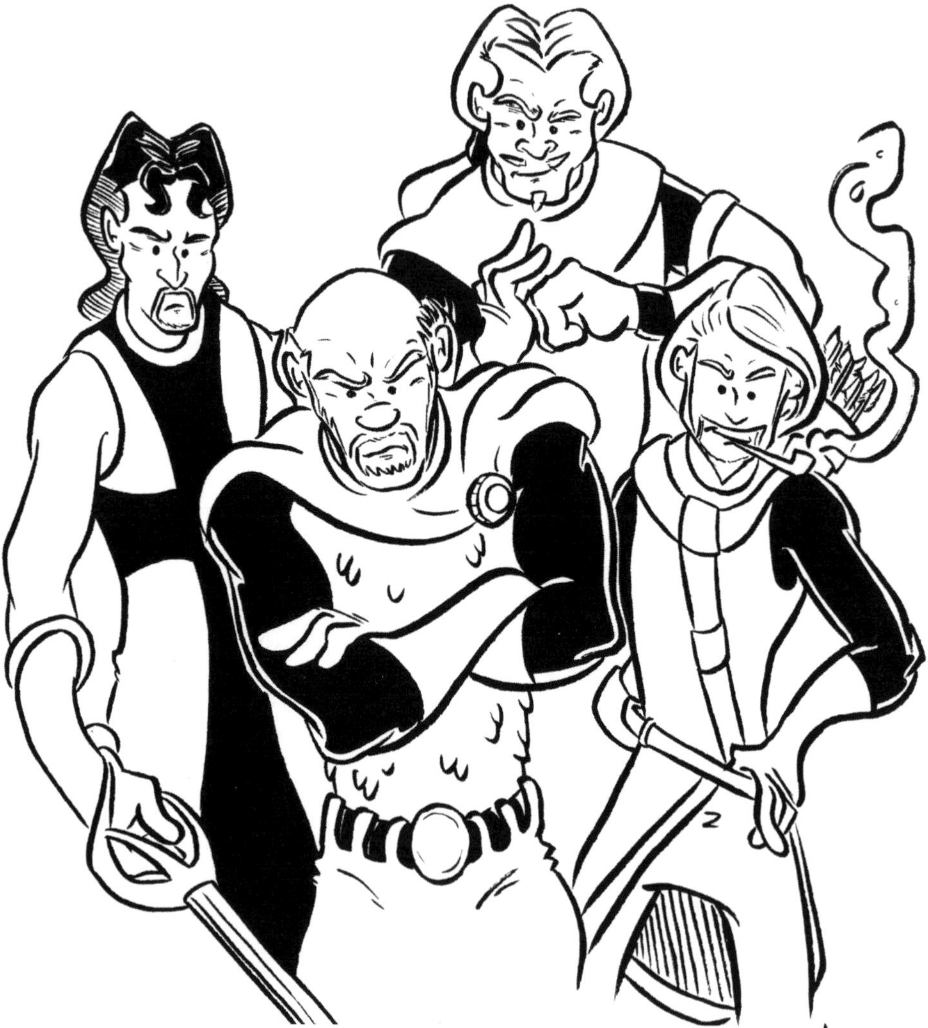
LEX!

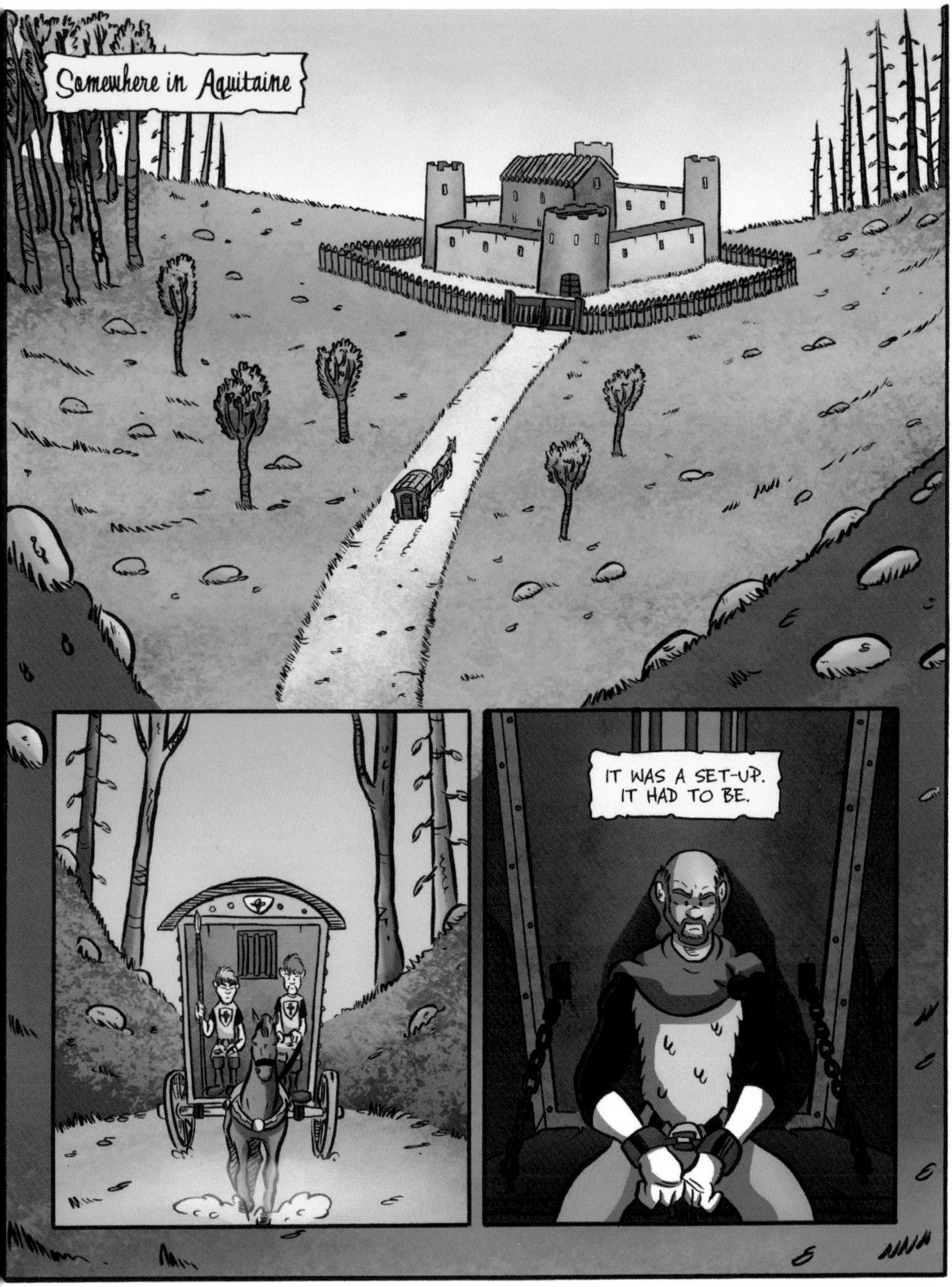
Somewhere in Aquitaine
IT WAS A SET-UP. IT HAD TO BE.

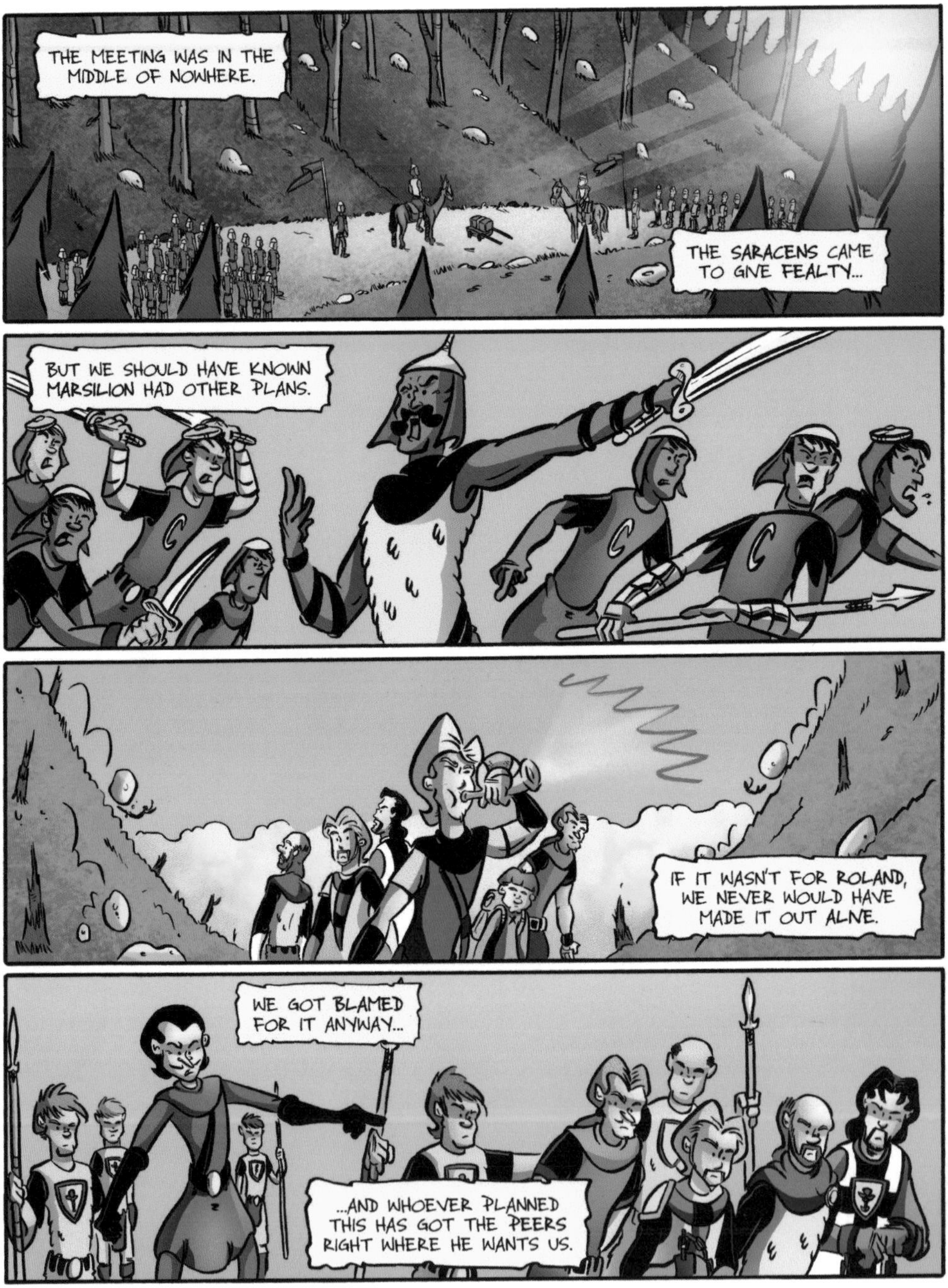
THE MEETING WAS IN THE MIDDLE OF NOWHERE.
THE SARACENS CAME TO GIVE FEALTY...
BUT WE SHOULD HAVE KNOWN MARSILION HAD OTHER PLANS.
IF IT WASN'T FOR ROLAND, WE NEVER WOULD HAVE MADE IT OUT ALIVE.
WE GOT BLAMED FOR IT ANYWAY...
...AND WHOEVER PLANNED THIS HAS GOT THE PEERS RIGHT WHERE HE WANTS US.

paladins tale

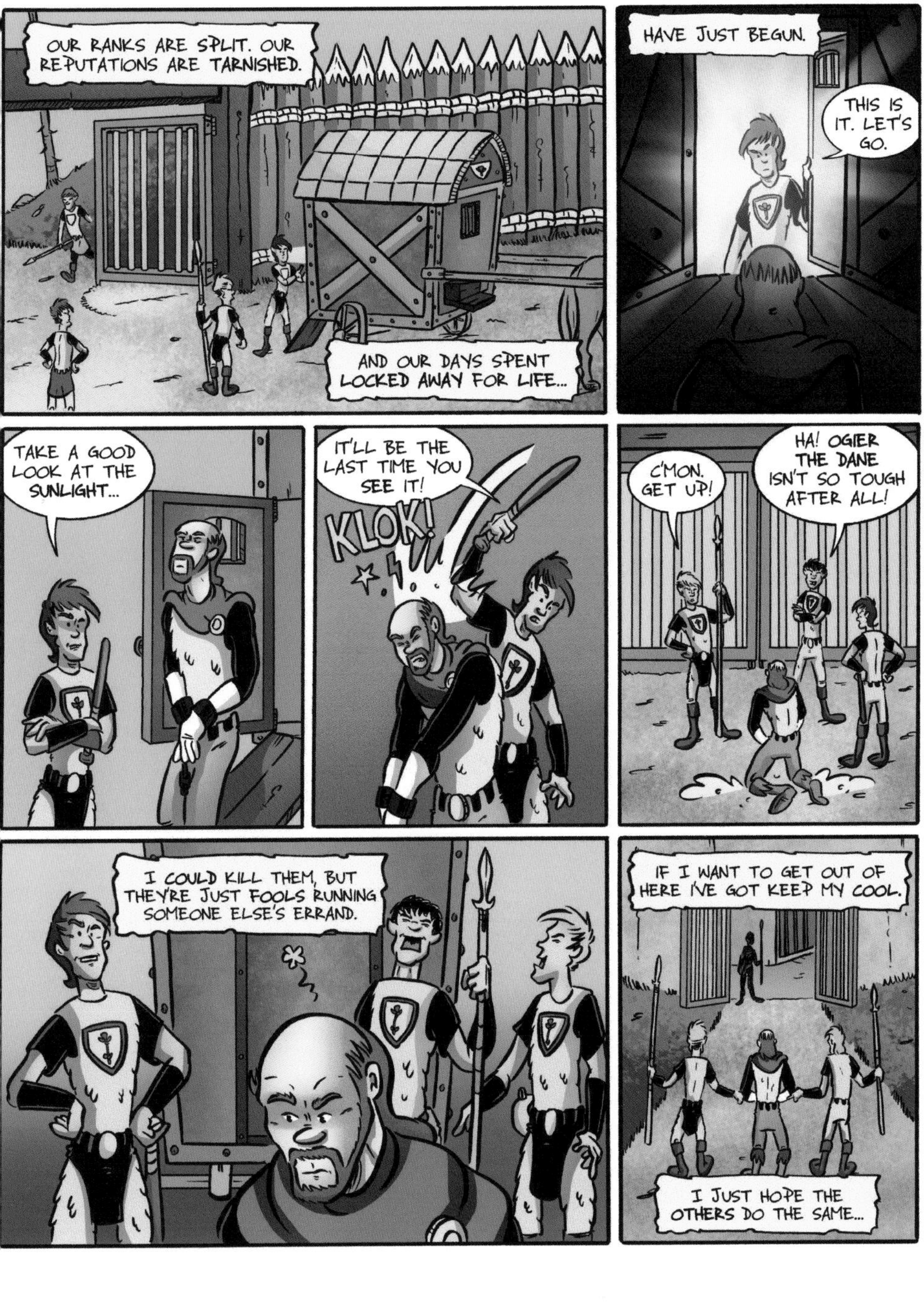
OUR RANKS ARE SPLIT. OUR REPUTATIONS ARE TARNISHED.
AND OUR DAYS SPENT LOCKED AWAY FOR LIFE...
HAVE JUST BEGUN.
THIS IS IT. LET'S GO.
TAKE A GOOD LOOK AT THE SUNLIGHT...
IT'LL BE THE LAST TIME YOU SEE IT!
KLOK!
C'MON. GET UP!
HA! OGIER THE DANE ISN'T SO TOUGH AFTER ALL!
I COULD KILL THEM, BUT THEY'RE JUST FOOLS RUNNING SOMEONE ELSE'S ERRAND.
IF I WANT TO GET OUT OF HERE I'VE GOT KEEP MY COOL.
I JUST HOPE THE OTHERS DO THE SAME...

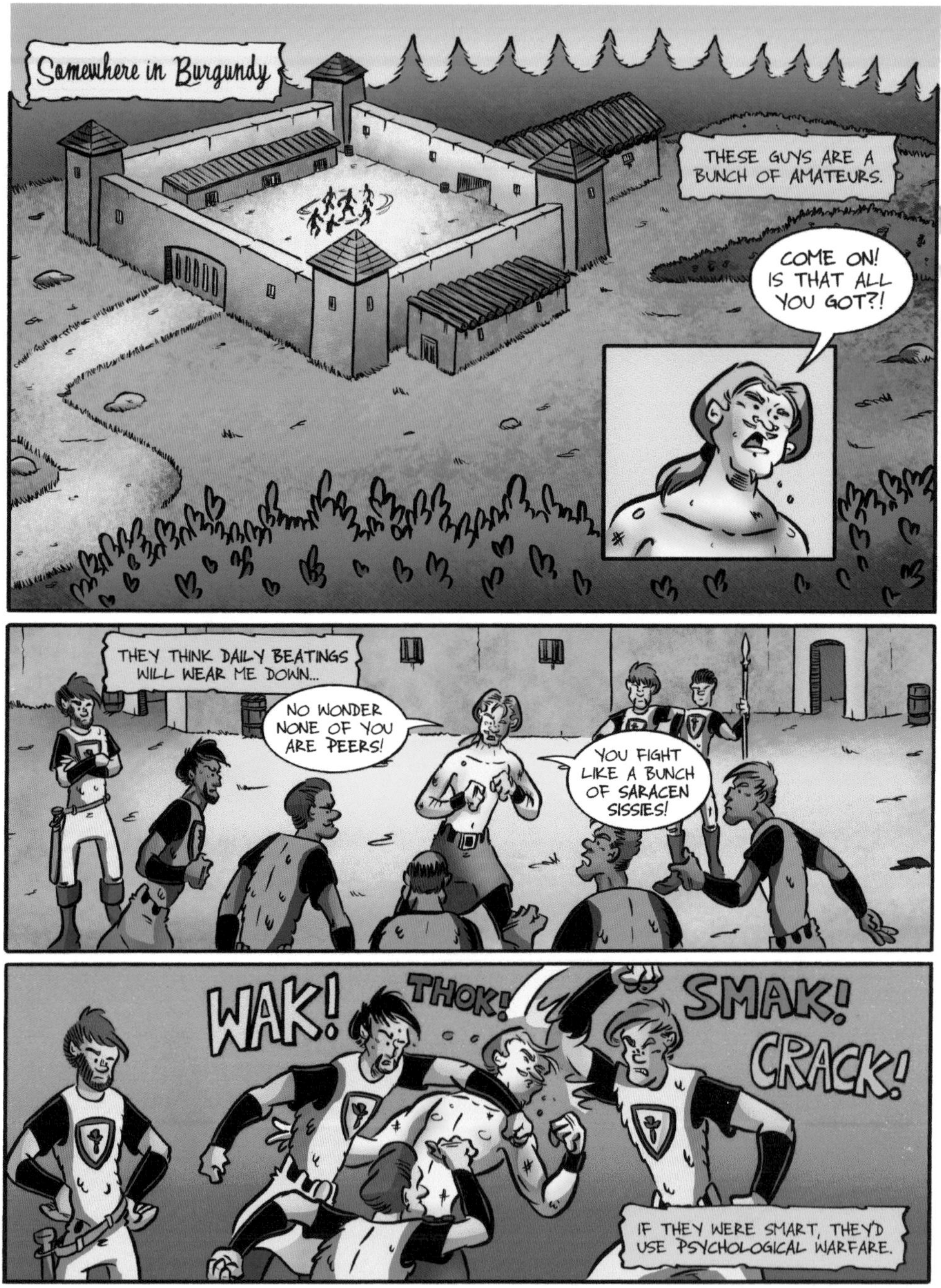
Somewhere in Burgundy
THESE GUYS ARE A BUNCH OF AMATEURS.
COME ON! IS THAT ALL YOU GOT?!
THEY THINK DAILY BEATINGS WILL WEAR ME DOWN...
NO WONDER NONE OF YOU ARE PEERS!
YOU FIGHT LIKE A BUNCH OF SARACEN SISSIES!
WAK!
THOK!
SMAK!
CRACK!
IF THEY WERE SMART, THEY'D USE PSYCHOLOGICAL WARFARE.

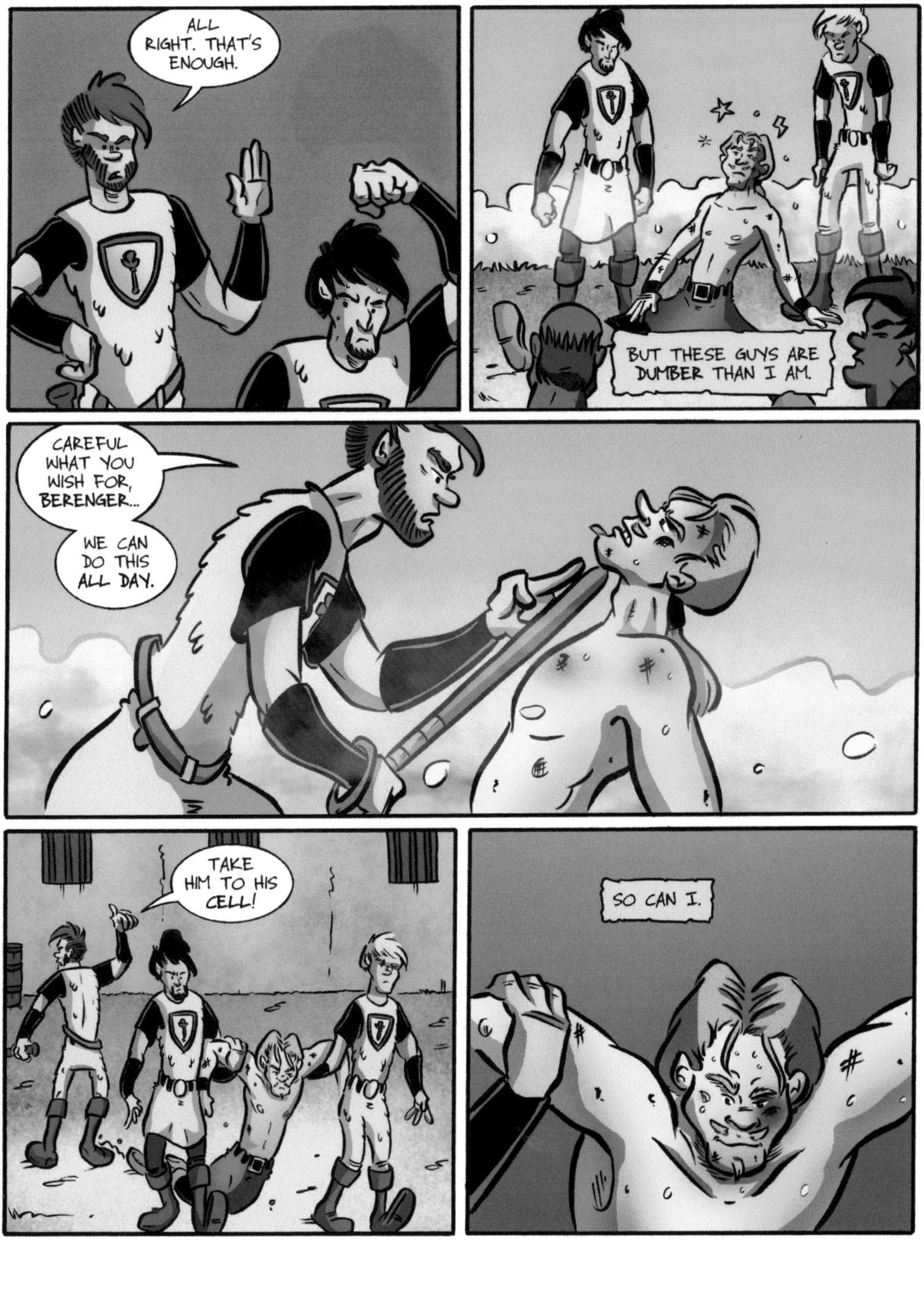
ALL RIGHT. THAT'S ENOUGH.
BUT THESE GUYS ARE DUMBER THAN I AM.
CAREFUL WHAT YOU WISH FOR, BERENGER...
WE CAN DO THIS ALL DAY.
TAKE HIM TO HIS CELL!
SO CAN I.

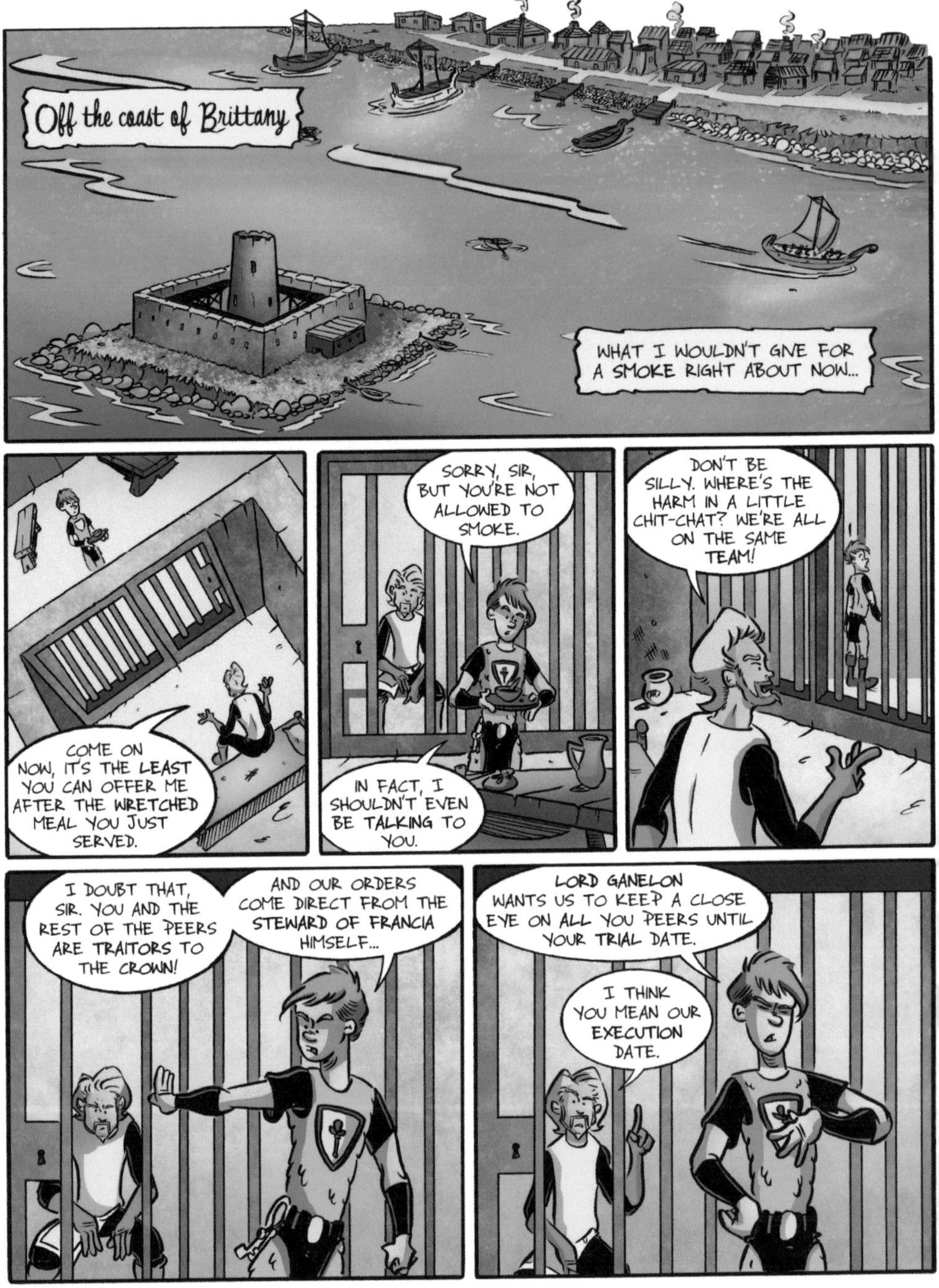
Off the coast of Brittany
WHAT I WOULDN'T GIVE FOR A SMOKE RIGHT ABOUT NOW...
COME ON NOW, IT'S THE LEAST YOU CAN OFFER ME AFTER THE WRETCHED MEAL YOU JUST SERVED.
SORRY, SIR, BUT YOU'RE NOT ALLOWED TO SMOKE.
IN FACT, I SHOULDN'T EVEN BE TALKING TO YOU.
DON'T BE SILLY. WHERE'S THE HARM IN A LITTLE CHIT-CHAT? WE'RE ALL ON THE SAME TEAM!
I DOUBT THAT, SIR. YOU AND THE REST OF THE PEERS ARE TRAITORS TO THE CROWN!
AND OUR ORDERS COME DIRECT FROM THE STEWARD OF FRANCIA HIMSELF...
LORD GANELON WANTS US TO KEEP A CLOSE EYE ON ALL YOU PEERS UNTIL YOUR TRIAL DATE.
I THINK YOU MEAN OUR EXECUTION DATE.

paladins tale

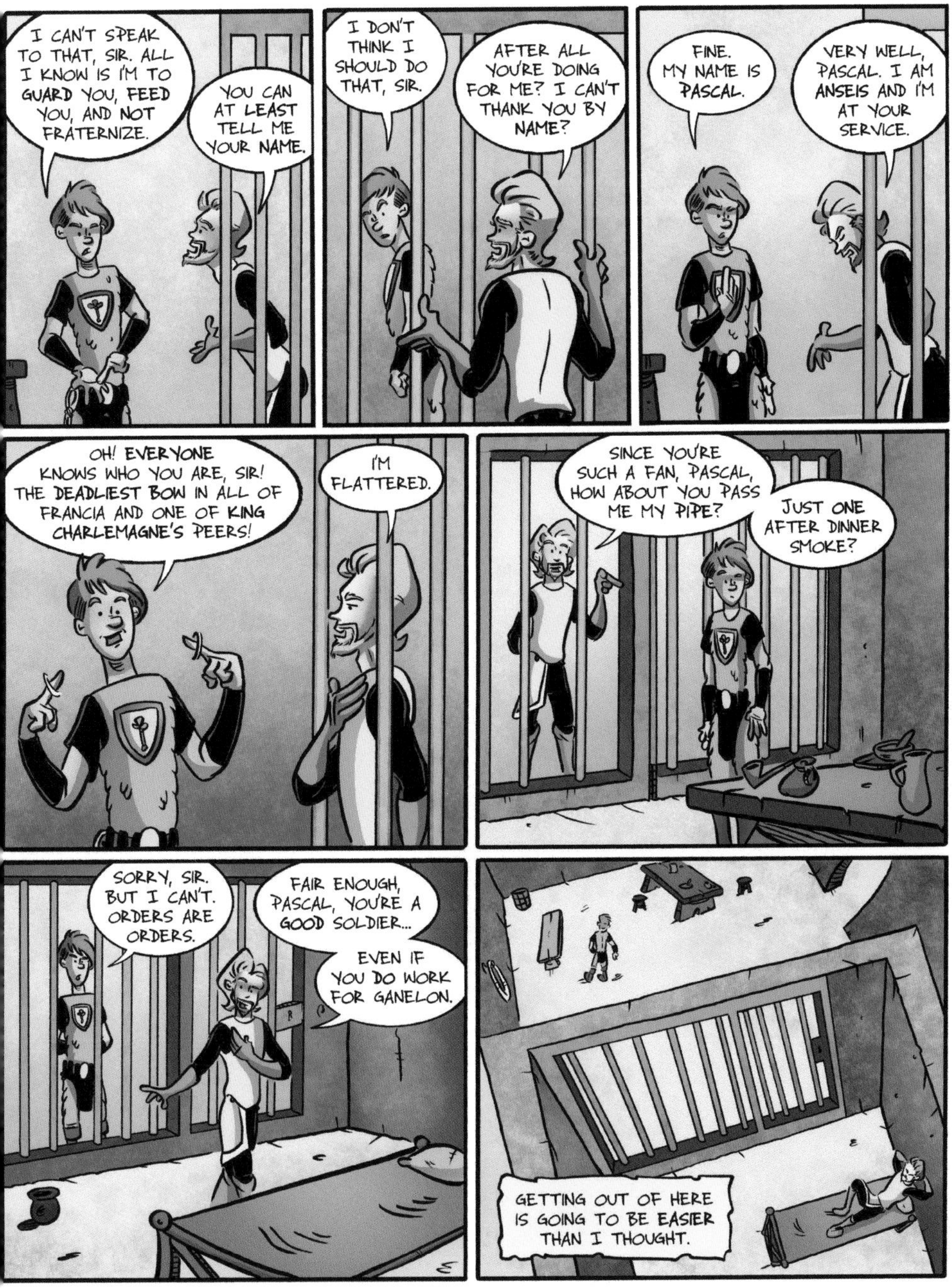
I CAN'T SPEAK TO THAT, SIR. ALL I KNOW IS I'M TO GUARD YOU, FEED YOU, AND NOT FRATERNIZE.
YOU CAN AT LEAST TELL ME YOUR NAME.
I DON'T THINK I SHOULD DO THAT, SIR.
AFTER ALL YOU'RE DOING FOR ME? I CAN'T THANK YOU BY NAME?
FINE. MY NAME IS PASCAL.
VERY WELL, PASCAL. I AM ANSEIS AND I'M AT YOUR SERVICE.
OH! EVERYONE KNOWS WHO YOU ARE, SIR! THE DEADLIEST BOW IN ALL OF FRANCIA AND ONE OF KING CHARLEMAGNE'S PEERS!
I'M FLATTERED.
SINCE YOU'RE SUCH A FAN, PASCAL, HOW ABOUT YOU PASS ME MY PIPE?
JUST ONE AFTER DINNER SMOKE?
SORRY, SIR. BUT I CAN'T. ORDERS ARE ORDERS.
FAIR ENOUGH, PASCAL, YOU'RE A GOOD SOLDIER...
EVEN IF YOU DO WORK FOR GANELON.
GETTING OUT OF HERE IS GOING TO BE EASIER THAN I THOUGHT.

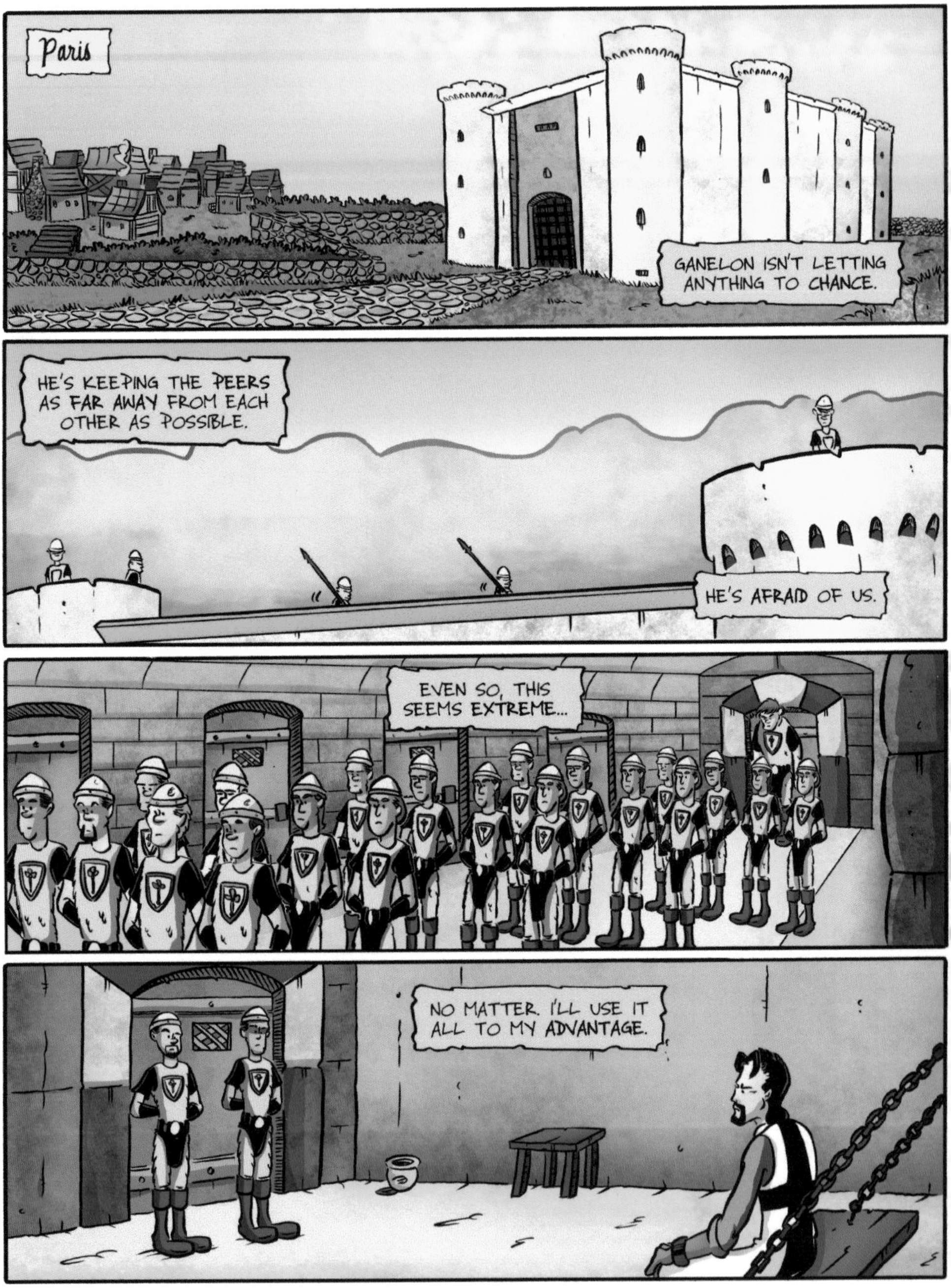
Paris
GANELON ISN'T LETTING ANYTHING TO CHANCE.
HE'S KEEPING THE PEERS AS FAR AWAY FROM EACH OTHER AS POSSIBLE.
HE'S AFRAID OF US.
EVEN SO, THIS SEEMS EXTREME...
NO MATTER. I'LL USE IT ALL TO MY ADVANTAGE.

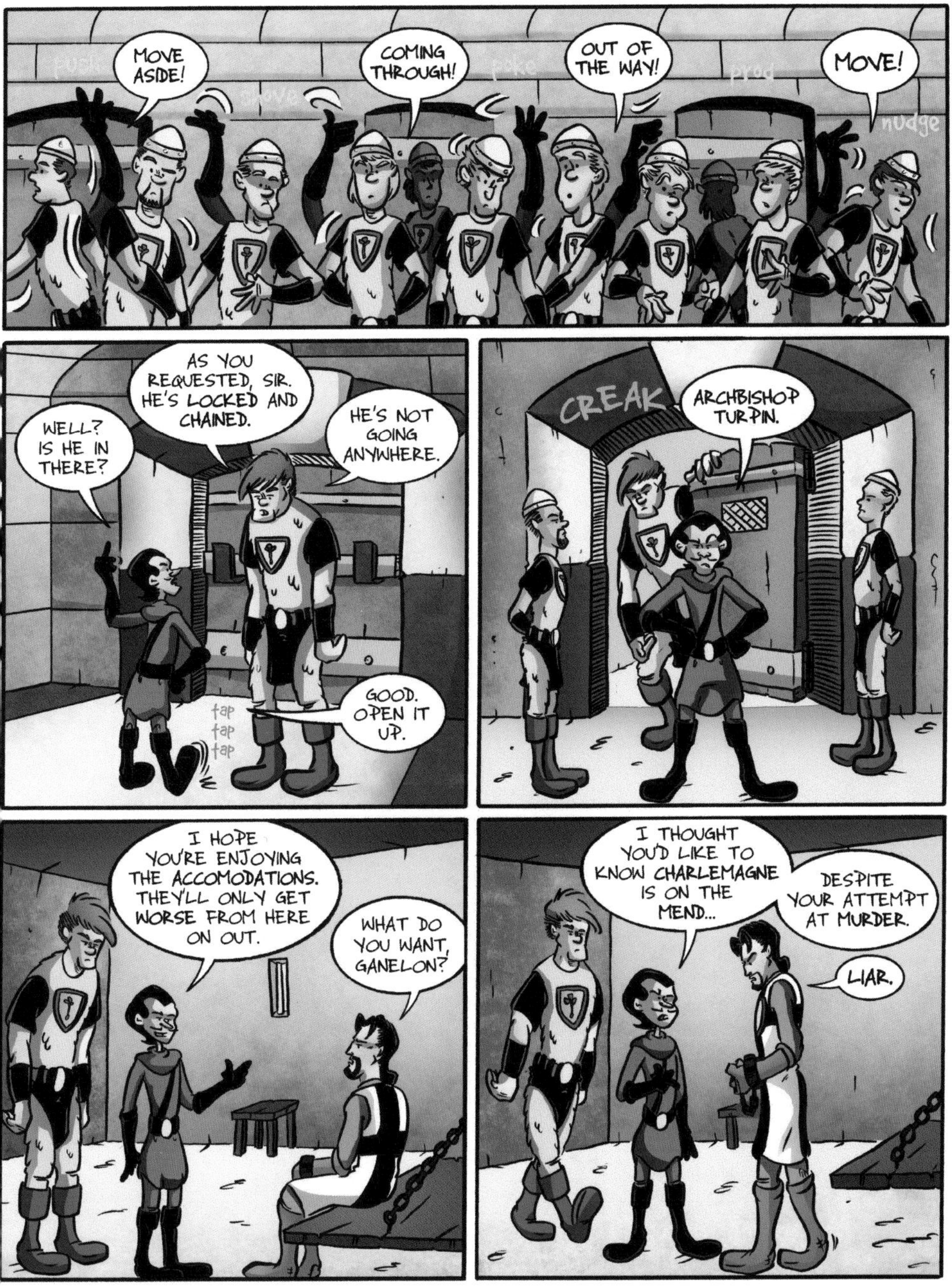
push
MOVE ASIDE!
shove
COMING THROUGH!
poke
OUT OF THE WAY!
prod
MOVE!
nudge
WELL? IS HE IN THERE?
AS YOU REQUESTED, SIR. HE'S LOCKED AND CHAINED.
HE'S NOT GOING ANYWHERE.
tap tap tap
GOOD. OPEN IT UP.
CREAK
ARCHBISHOP TURPIN.
I HOPE YOU'RE ENJOYING THE ACCOMODATIONS. THEY'LL ONLY GET WORSE FROM HERE ON OUT.
WHAT DO YOU WANT, GANELON?
I THOUGHT YOU'D LIKE TO KNOW CHARLEMAGNE IS ON THE MEND...
DESPITE YOUR ATTEMPT AT MURDER.
LIAR.

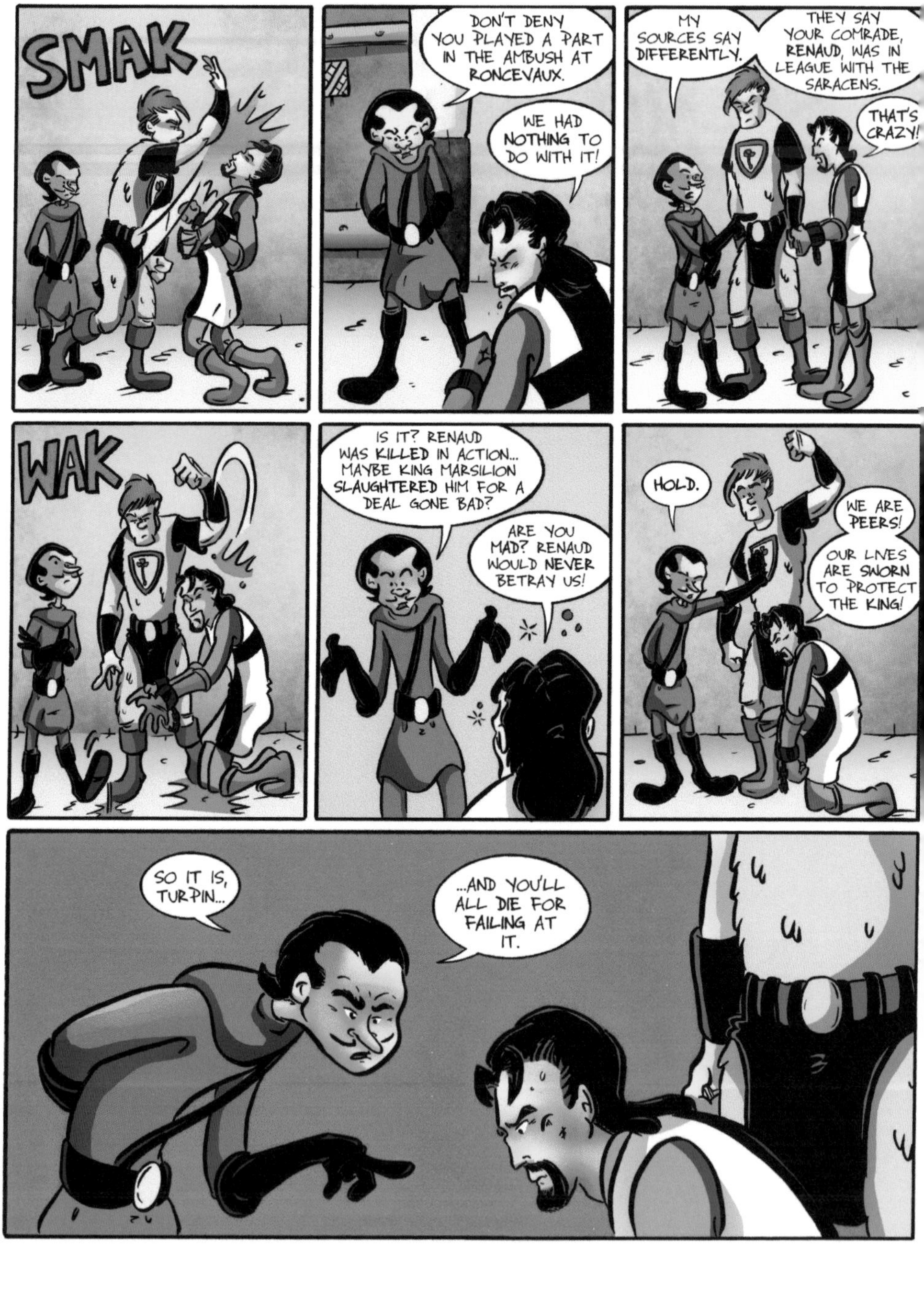
SMAK
DON'T DENY YOU PLAYED A PART IN THE AMBUSH AT RONCEVAUX.
WE HAD NOTHING TO DO WITH IT!
MY SOURCES SAY DIFFERENTLY.
THEY SAY YOUR COMRADE, RENAUD, WAS IN LEAGUE WITH THE SARACENS.
THAT'S CRAZY!
WAK
IS IT? RENAUD WAS KILLED IN ACTION... MAYBE KING MARSILION SLAUGHTERED HIM FOR A DEAL GONE BAD?
ARE YOU MAD? RENAUD WOULD NEVER BETRAY US!
HOLD.
WE ARE PEERS!
OUR LIVES ARE SWORN TO PROTECT THE KING!
SO IT IS, TURPIN...
...AND YOU'LL ALL DIE FOR FAILING AT IT.

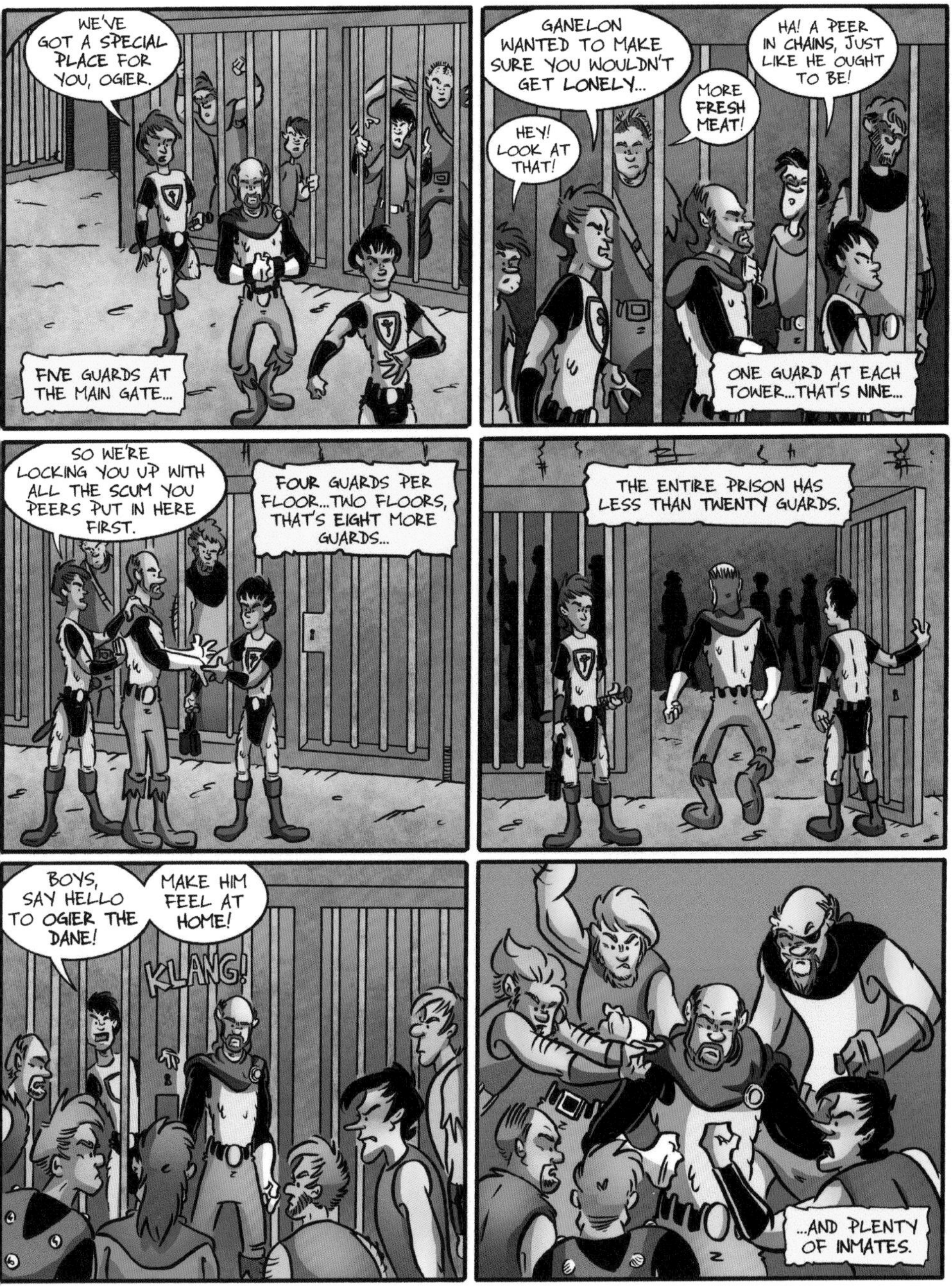
WE'VE GOT A SPECIAL PLACE FOR YOU, OGIER.
FIVE GUARDS AT THE MAIN GATE...
GANELON WANTED TO MAKE SURE YOU WOULDN'T GET LONELY...
HA! A PEER IN CHAINS, JUST LIKE HE OUGHT TO BE!
MORE FRESH MEAT!
HEY! LOOK AT THAT!
ONE GUARD AT EACH TOWER...THAT'S NINE...
SO WE'RE LOCKING YOU UP WITH ALL THE SCUM YOU PEERS PUT IN HERE FIRST.
FOUR GUARDS PER FLOOR...TWO FLOORS, THAT'S EIGHT MORE GUARDS...
THE ENTIRE PRISON HAS LESS THAN TWENTY GUARDS.
BOYS, SAY HELLO TO OGIER THE DANE!
MAKE HIM FEEL AT HOME!
KLANG!
...AND PLENTY OF INMATES.

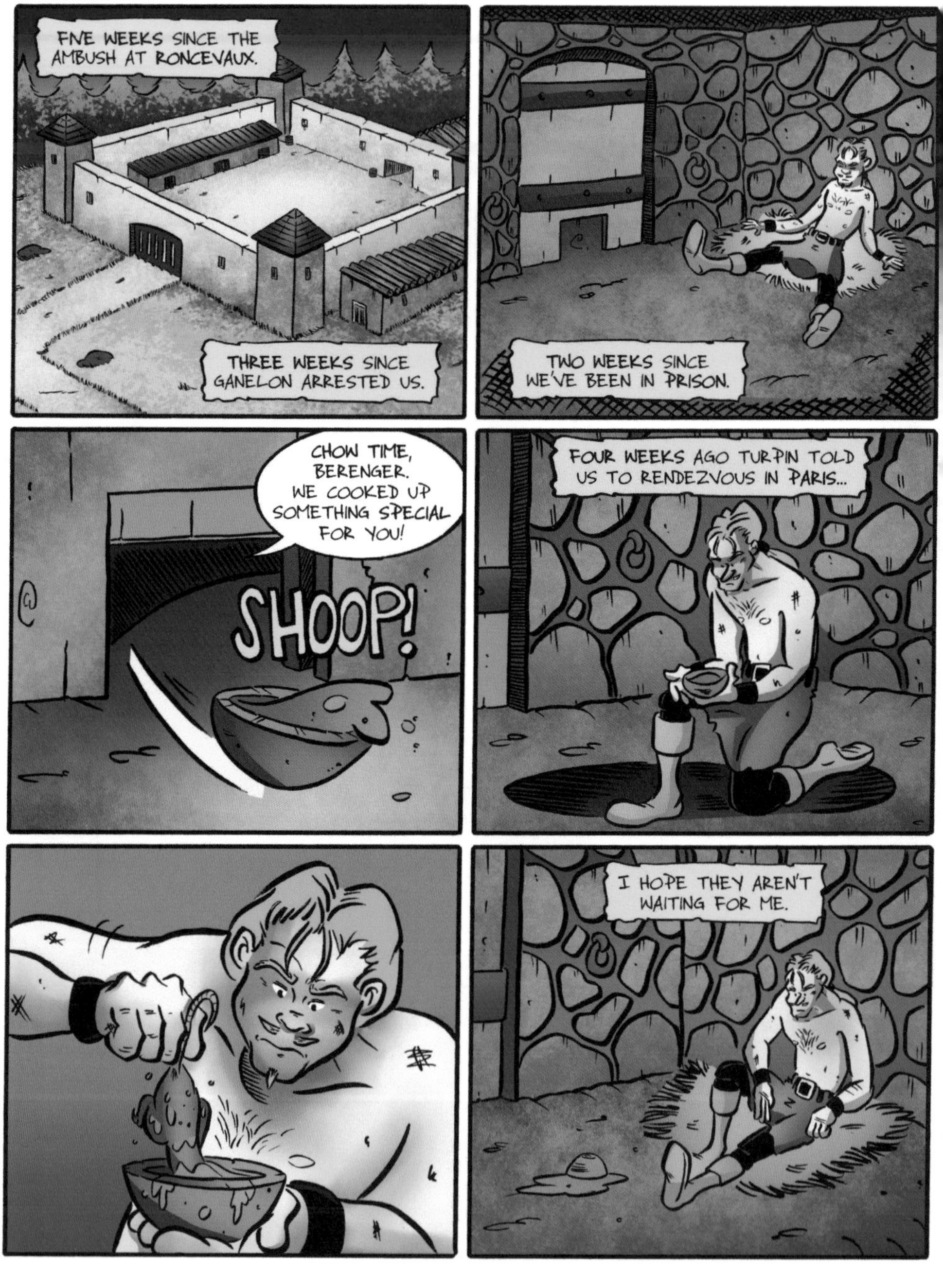
FIVE WEEKS SINCE THE AMBUSH AT RONCEVAUX.
THREE WEEKS SINCE GANELON ARRESTED US.
TWO WEEKS SINCE WE'VE BEEN IN PRISON.
CHOW TIME, BERENGER. WE COOKED UP SOMETHING SPECIAL FOR YOU!
SHOOP!
FOUR WEEKS AGO TURPIN TOLD US TO RENDEZVOUS IN PARIS...
I HOPE THEY AREN'T WAITING FOR ME.

paladins tale

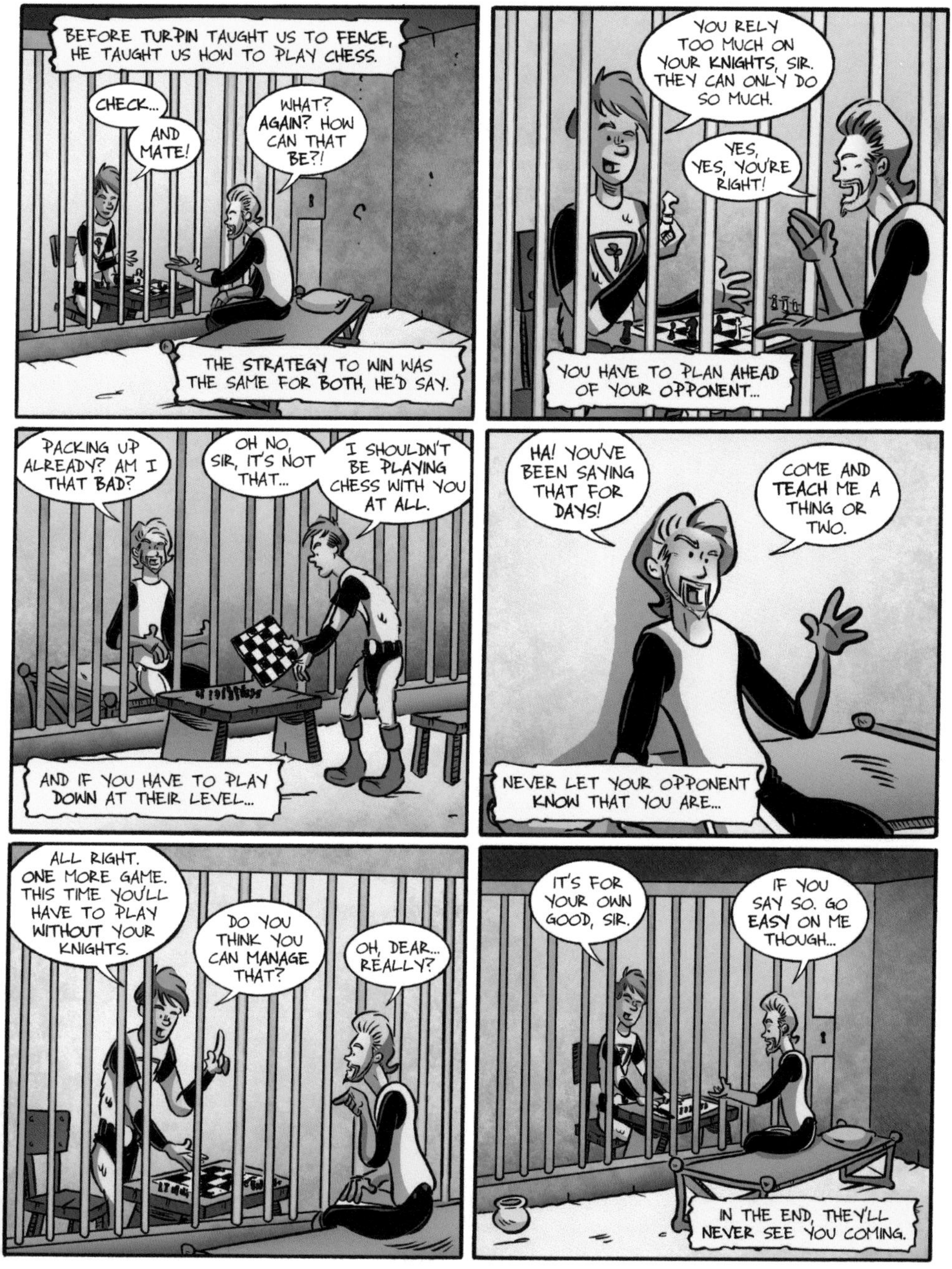
BEFORE TURPIN TAUGHT US TO FENCE, HE TAUGHT US HOW TO PLAY CHESS.
CHECK...
AND MATE!
WHAT? AGAIN? HOW CAN THAT BE?!
THE STRATEGY TO WIN WAS THE SAME FOR BOTH, HE'D SAY.
YOU RELY TOO MUCH ON YOUR KNIGHTS, SIR. THEY CAN ONLY DO SO MUCH.
YES, YES, YOU'RE RIGHT!
YOU HAVE TO PLAN AHEAD OF YOUR OPPONENT...
PACKING UP ALREADY? AM I THAT BAD?
OH NO, SIR, IT'S NOT THAT...
I SHOULDN'T BE PLAYING CHESS WITH YOU AT ALL.
AND IF YOU HAVE TO PLAY DOWN AT THEIR LEVEL...
HA! YOU'VE BEEN SAYING THAT FOR DAYS!
COME AND TEACH ME A THING OR TWO.
NEVER LET YOUR OPPONENT KNOW THAT YOU ARE...
ALL RIGHT. ONE MORE GAME. THIS TIME YOU'LL HAVE TO PLAY WITHOUT YOUR KNIGHTS.
DO YOU THINK YOU CAN MANAGE THAT?
OH, DEAR... REALLY?
IT'S FOR YOUR OWN GOOD, SIR.
IF YOU SAY SO. GO EASY ON ME THOUGH...
IN THE END, THEY'LL NEVER SEE YOU COMING.

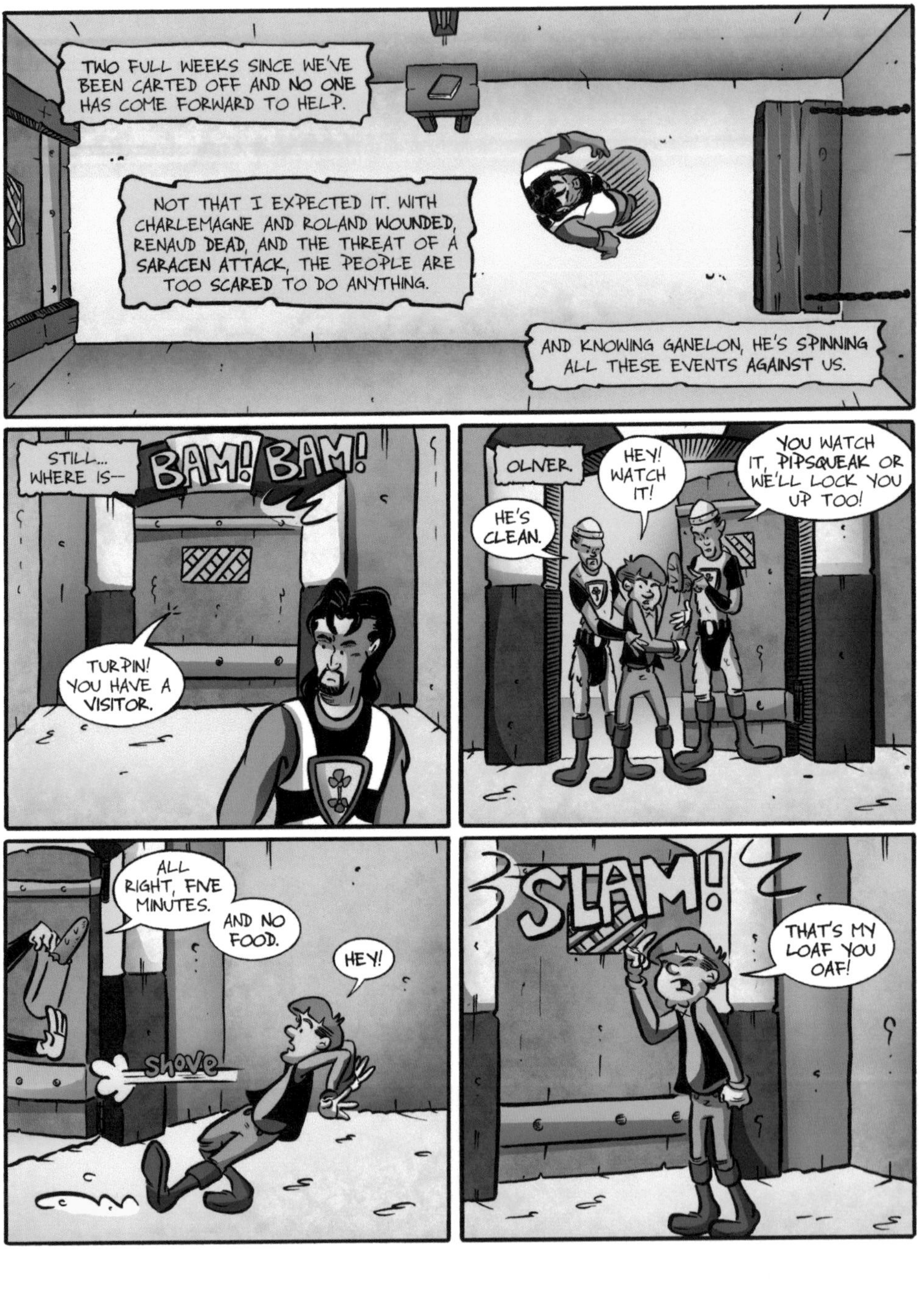
TWO FULL WEEKS SINCE WE'VE BEEN CARTED OFF AND NO ONE HAS COME FORWARD TO HELP.
NOT THAT I EXPECTED IT. WITH CHARLEMAGNE AND ROLAND WOUNDED, RENAUD DEAD, AND THE THREAT OF A SARACEN ATTACK, THE PEOPLE ARE TOO SCARED TO DO ANYTHING.
AND KNOWING GANELON, HE'S SPINNING ALL THESE EVENTS AGAINST US.
STILL... WHERE IS--
BAM! BAM!
TURPIN! YOU HAVE A VISITOR.
OLIVER.
HE'S CLEAN.
HEY! WATCH IT!
YOU WATCH IT, PIPSQUEAK OR WE'LL LOCK YOU UP TOO!
ALL RIGHT, FIVE MINUTES.
AND NO FOOD.
HEY!
shove
SLAM!
THAT'S MY LOAF YOU OAF!

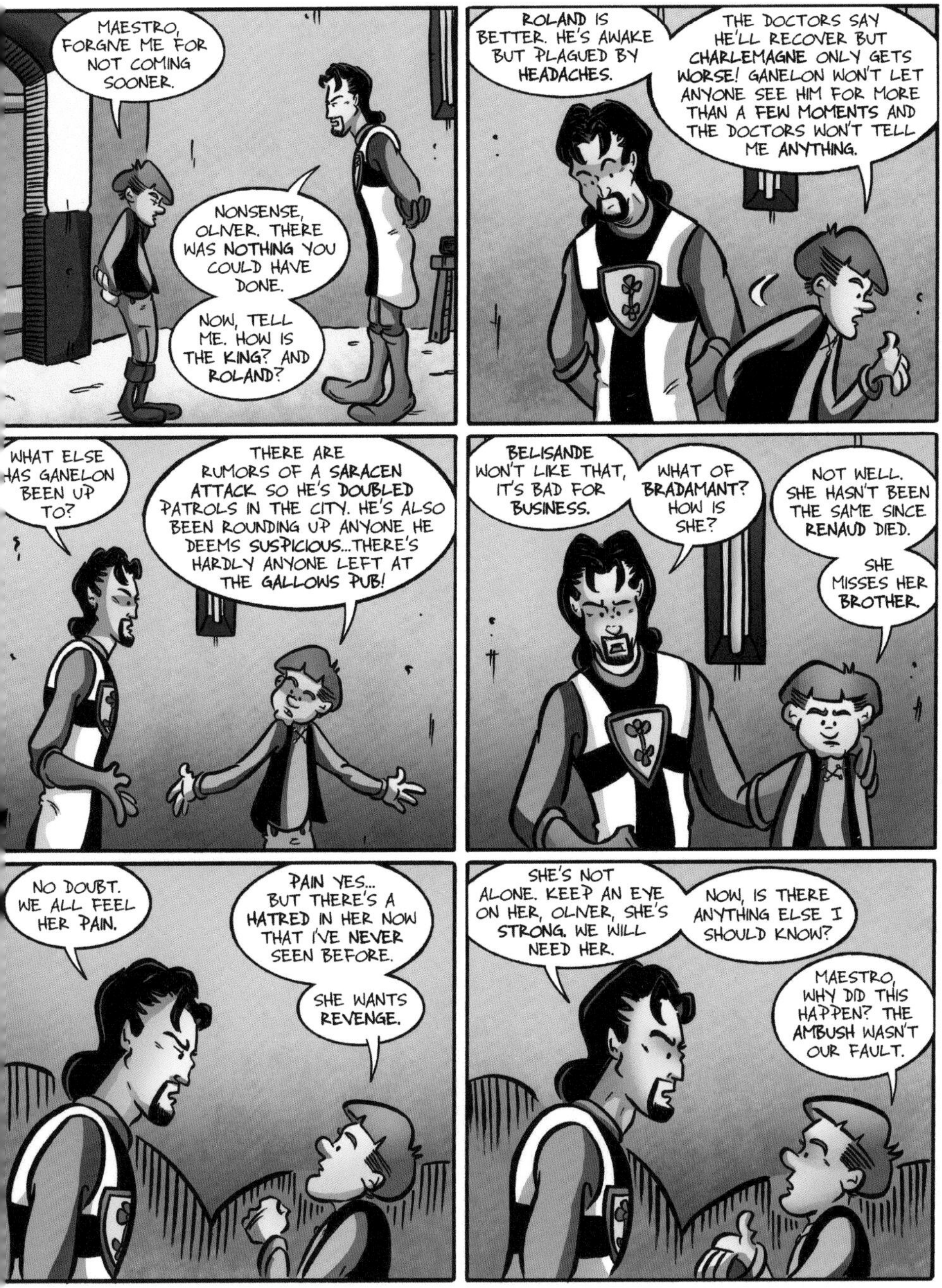

MAESTRO, FORGIVE ME FOR NOT COMING SOONER.
NONSENSE, OLIVER. THERE WAS NOTHING YOU COULD HAVE DONE.
NOW, TELL ME. HOW IS THE KING? AND ROLAND?
ROLAND IS BETTER. HE'S AWAKE BUT PLAGUED BY HEADACHES.
THE DOCTORS SAY HE'LL RECOVER BUT CHARLEMAGNE ONLY GETS WORSE! GANELON WON'T LET ANYONE SEE HIM FOR MORE THAN A FEW MOMENTS AND THE DOCTORS WON'T TELL ME ANYTHING.
WHAT ELSE HAS GANELON BEEN UP TO?
THERE ARE RUMORS OF A SARACEN ATTACK SO HE'S DOUBLED PATROLS IN THE CITY. HE'S ALSO BEEN ROUNDING UP ANYONE HE DEEMS SUSPICIOUS...THERE'S HARDLY ANYONE LEFT AT THE GALLOWS PUB!
BELISANDE WON'T LIKE THAT, IT'S BAD FOR BUSINESS.
WHAT OF BRADAMANT? HOW IS SHE?
NOT WELL. SHE HASN'T BEEN THE SAME SINCE RENAUD DIED.
SHE MISSES HER BROTHER.
NO DOUBT. WE ALL FEEL HER PAIN.
PAIN YES... BUT THERE'S A HATRED IN HER NOW THAT I'VE NEVER SEEN BEFORE.
SHE WANTS REVENGE.
SHE'S NOT ALONE. KEEP AN EYE ON HER, OLIVER, SHE'S STRONG. WE WILL NEED HER.
NOW, IS THERE ANYTHING ELSE I SHOULD KNOW?
MAESTRO, WHY DID THIS HAPPEN? THE AMBUSH WASN'T OUR FAULT.

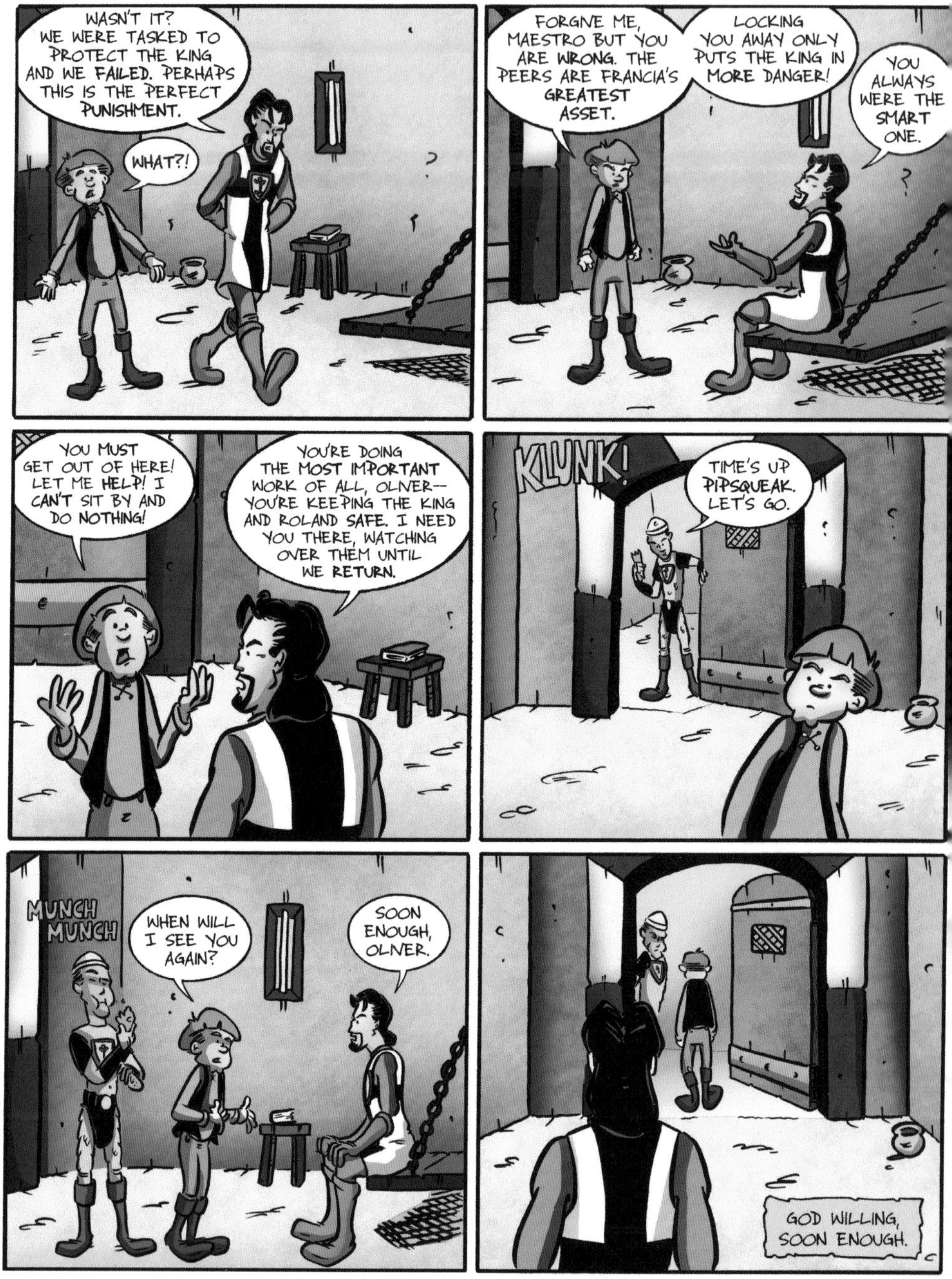
WASN'T IT? WE WERE TASKED TO PROTECT THE KING AND WE FAILED. PERHAPS THIS IS THE PERFECT PUNISHMENT.
WHAT?!
FORGIVE ME, MAESTRO BUT YOU ARE WRONG. THE PEERS ARE FRANCIA'S GREATEST ASSET.
LOCKING YOU AWAY ONLY PUTS THE KING IN MORE DANGER!
YOU ALWAYS WERE THE SMART ONE.
YOU MUST GET OUT OF HERE! LET ME HELP! I CAN'T SIT BY AND DO NOTHING!
YOU'RE DOING THE MOST IMPORTANT WORK OF ALL, OLIVER-- YOU'RE KEEPING THE KING AND ROLAND SAFE. I NEED YOU THERE, WATCHING OVER THEM UNTIL WE RETURN.
KLUNK!
TIME'S UP PIPSQUEAK. LET'S GO.
MUNCH MUNCH
WHEN WILL I SEE YOU AGAIN?
SOON ENOUGH, OLIVER.
GOD WILLING, SOON ENOUGH.

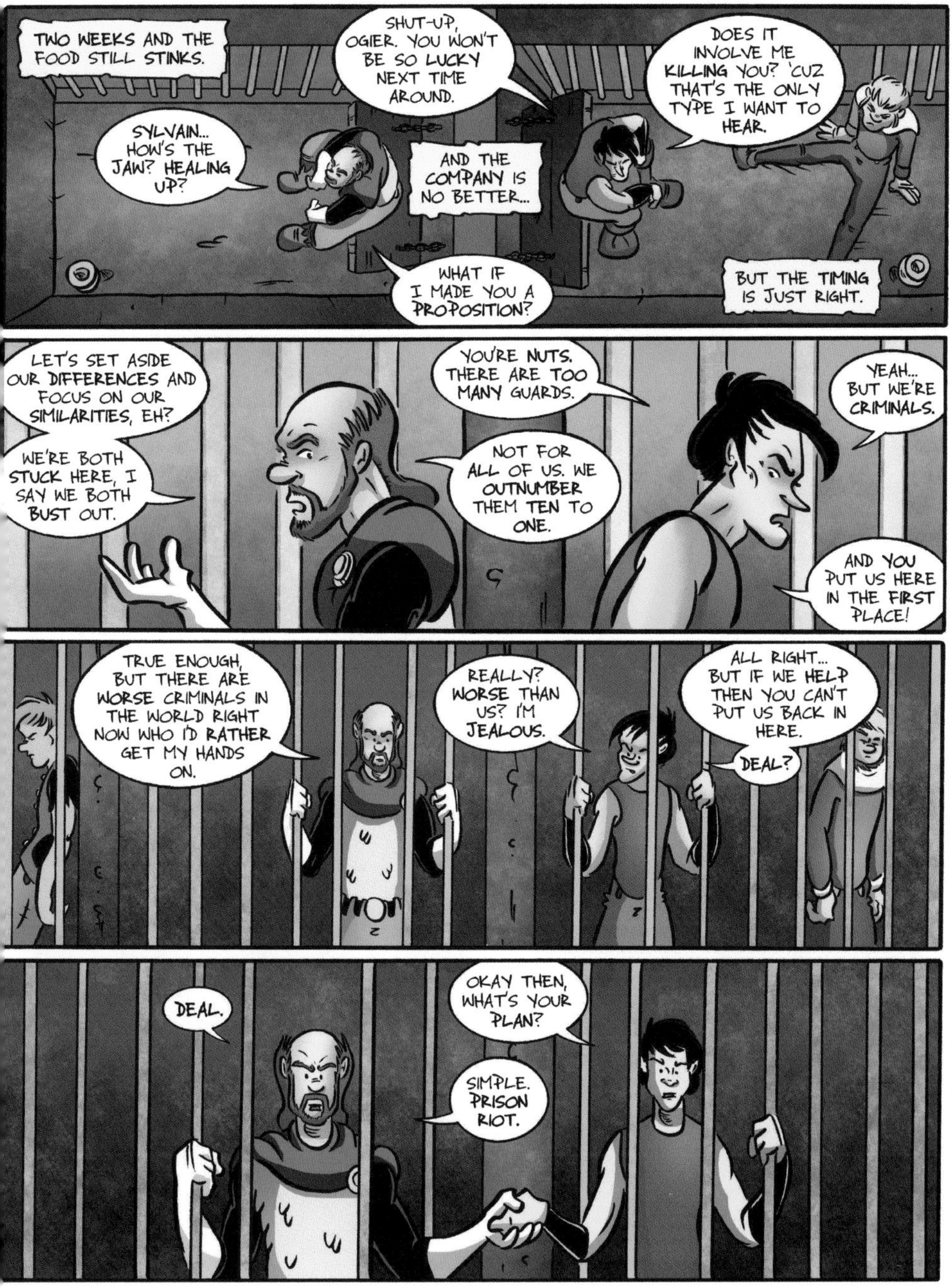
TWO WEEKS AND THE FOOD STILL STINKS.
SYLVAIN... HOW'S THE JAW? HEALING UP?
SHUT-UP, OGIER. YOU WON'T BE SO LUCKY NEXT TIME AROUND.
AND THE COMPANY IS NO BETTER...
WHAT IF I MADE YOU A PROPOSITION?
DOES IT INVOLVE ME KILLING YOU? 'CUZ THAT'S THE ONLY TYPE I WANT TO HEAR.
BUT THE TIMING IS JUST RIGHT.
LET'S SET ASIDE OUR DIFFERENCES AND FOCUS ON OUR SIMILARITIES, EH?
WE'RE BOTH STUCK HERE, I SAY WE BOTH BUST OUT.
YOU'RE NUTS. THERE ARE TOO MANY GUARDS.
NOT FOR ALL OF US. WE OUTNUMBER THEM TEN TO ONE.
YEAH... BUT WE'RE CRIMINALS.
AND YOU PUT US HERE IN THE FIRST PLACE!
TRUE ENOUGH, BUT THERE ARE WORSE CRIMINALS IN THE WORLD RIGHT NOW WHO I'D RATHER GET MY HANDS ON.
REALLY? WORSE THAN US? I'M JEALOUS.
ALL RIGHT... BUT IF WE HELP THEN YOU CAN'T PUT US BACK IN HERE.
DEAL?
DEAL.
OKAY THEN, WHAT'S YOUR PLAN?
SIMPLE. PRISON RIOT.

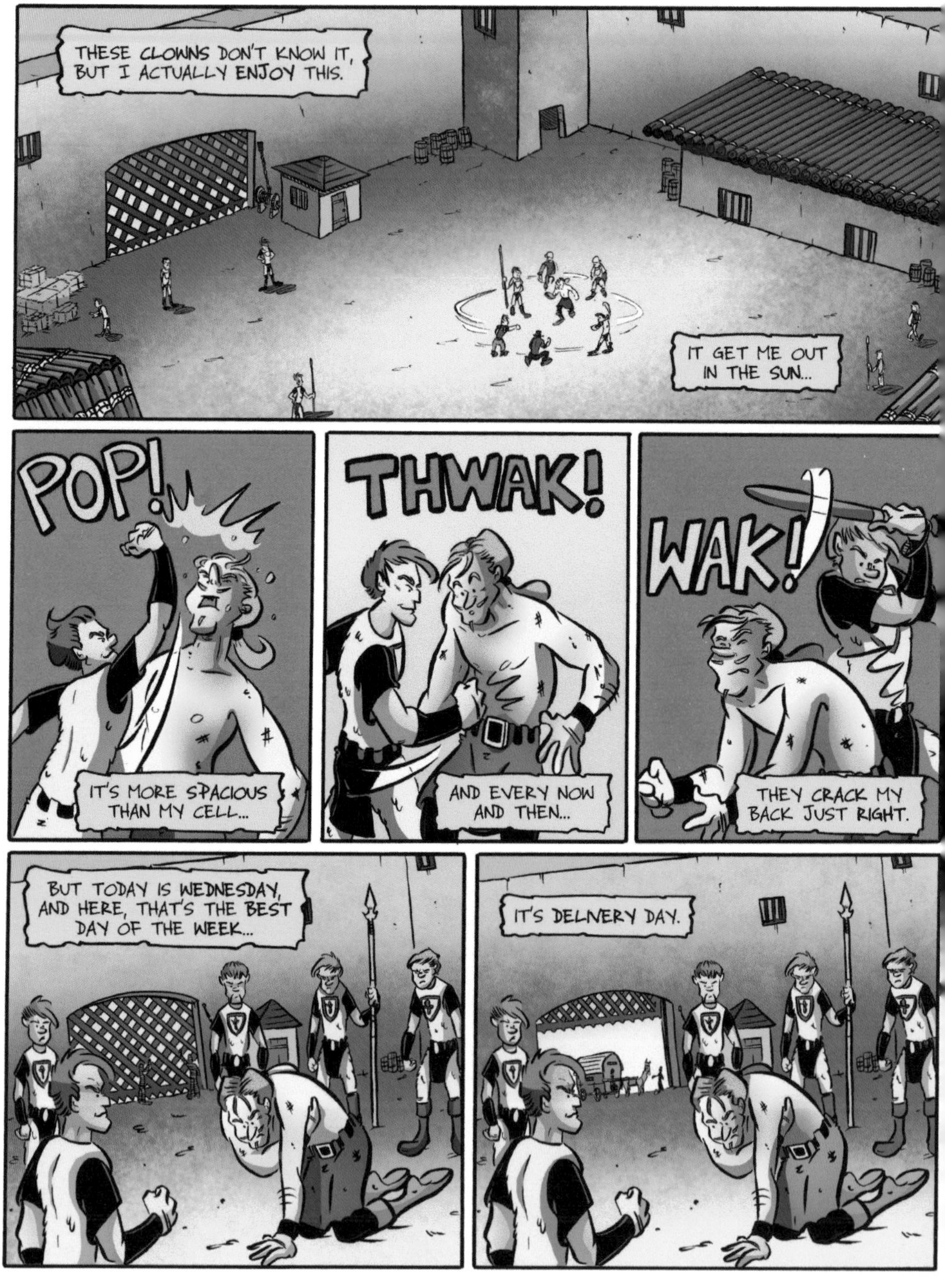
THESE CLOWNS DON'T KNOW IT, BUT I ACTUALLY ENJOY THIS.
IT GET ME OUT IN THE SUN...
POP!
IT'S MORE SPACIOUS THAN MY CELL...
THWAK!
AND EVERY NOW AND THEN...
WAK!
THEY CRACK MY BACK JUST RIGHT.
BUT TODAY IS WEDNESDAY, AND HERE, THAT'S THE BEST DAY OF THE WEEK...
IT'S DELIVERY DAY.

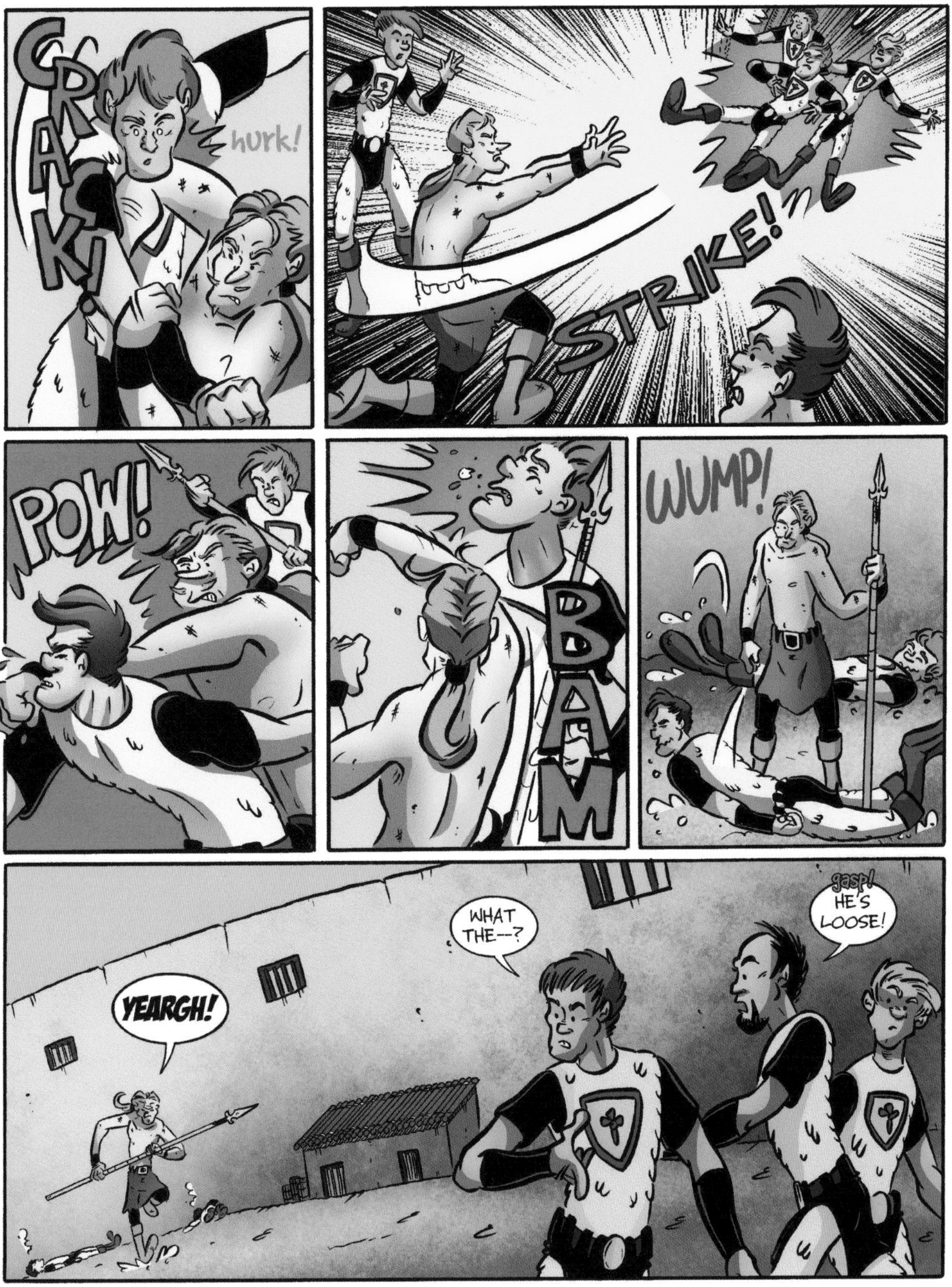
CRACK!
hurk!
STRIKE!
POW!
BAM
WUMP!
YEARGH!
WHAT THE--?
gasp!
HE'S LOOSE!

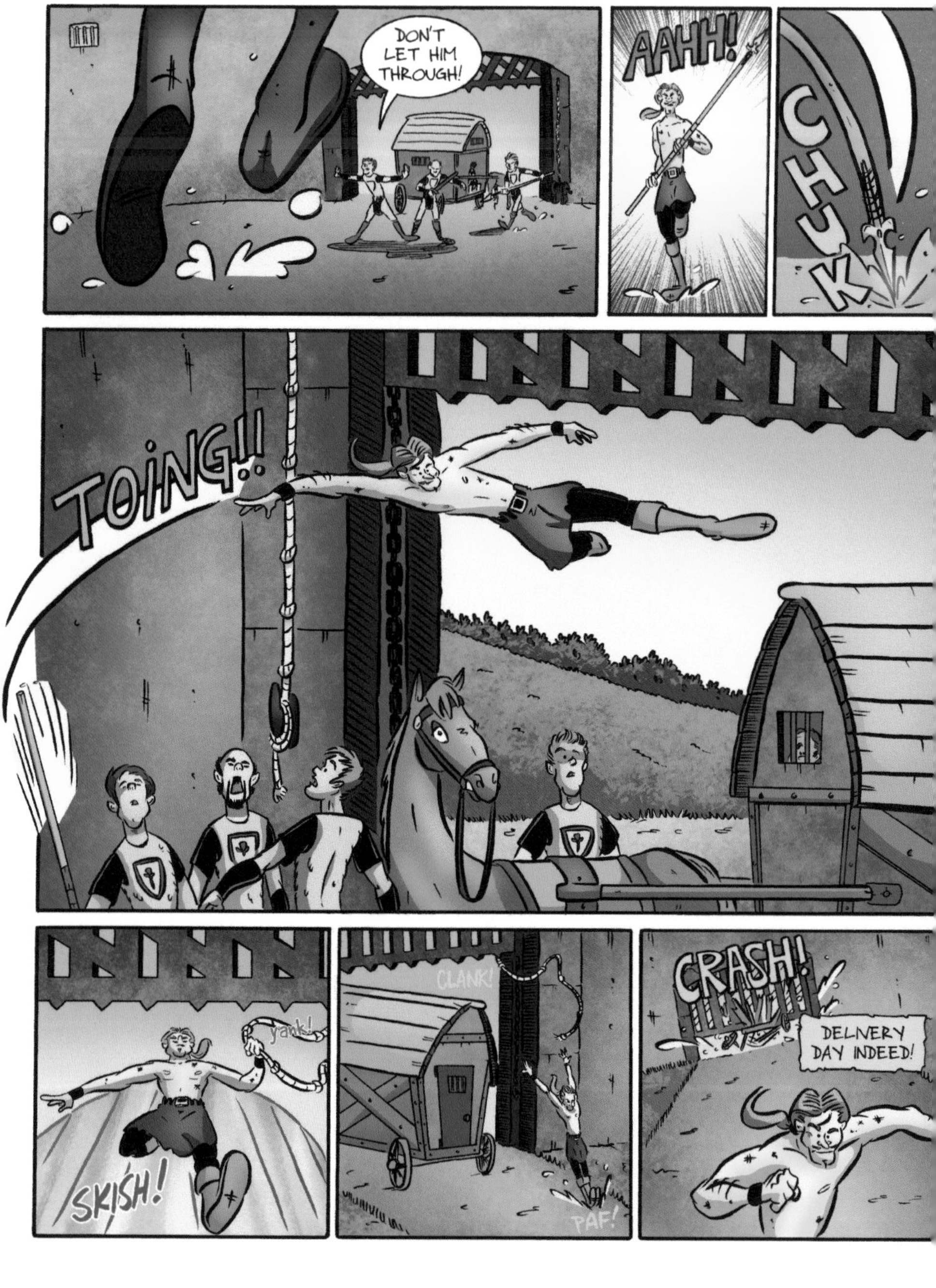
DON'T LET HIM THROUGH!
AAHH!
CHUK
TOING!!
yank!
SKISH!
CLANK!
PAF!
CRASH!
DELIVERY DAY INDEED!

paladins tale

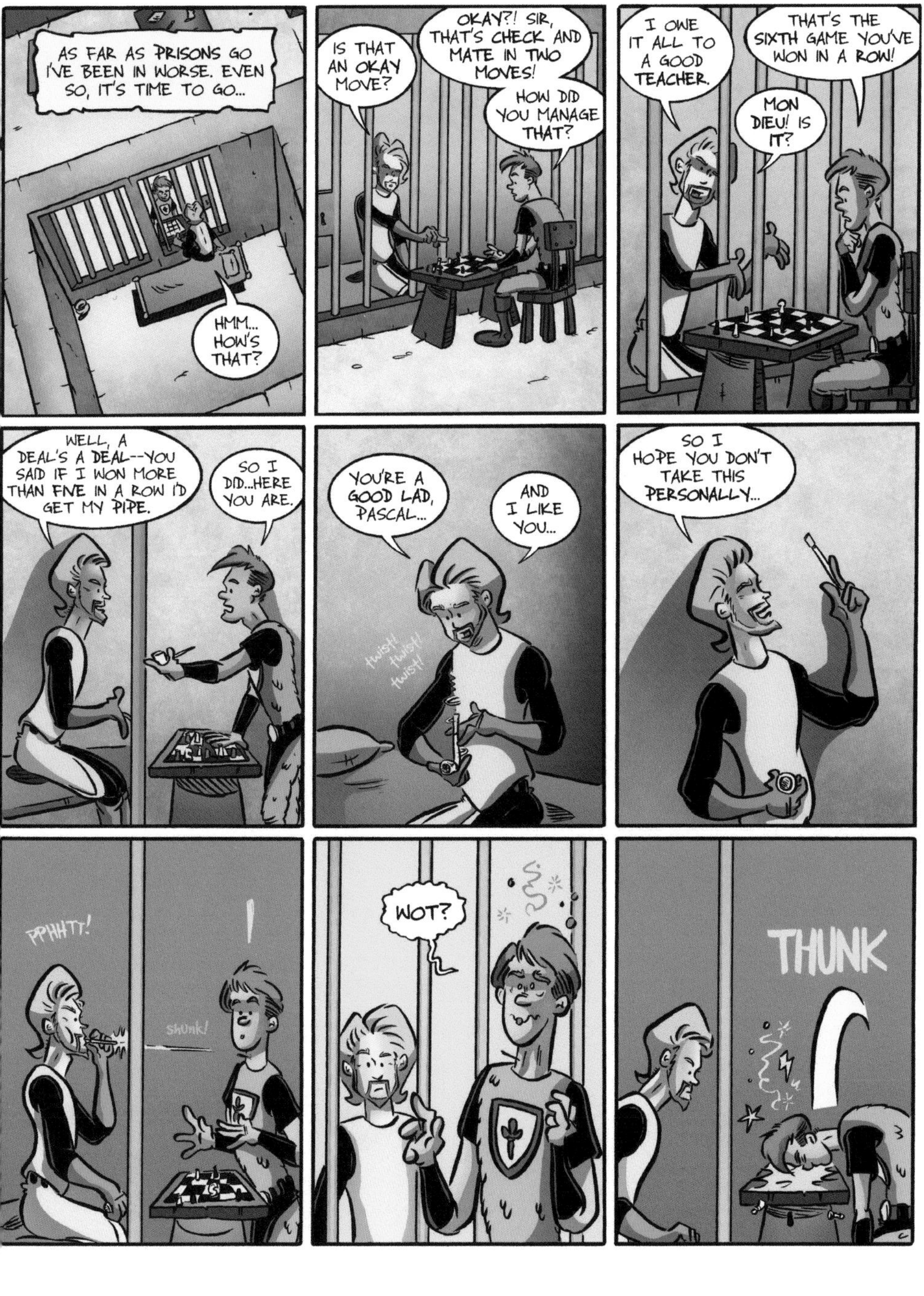
AS FAR AS PRISONS GO I'VE BEEN IN WORSE. EVEN SO, IT'S TIME TO GO...
HMM... HOW'S THAT?
IS THAT AN OKAY MOVE?
OKAY?! SIR, THAT'S CHECK AND MATE IN TWO MOVES!
HOW DID YOU MANAGE THAT?
I OWE IT ALL TO A GOOD TEACHER.
THAT'S THE SIXTH GAME YOU'VE WON IN A ROW!
MON DIEU! IS IT?
WELL, A DEAL'S A DEAL--YOU SAID IF I WON MORE THAN FIVE IN A ROW I'D GET MY PIPE.
SO I DID...HERE YOU ARE.
YOU'RE A GOOD LAD, PASCAL...
AND I LIKE YOU...
twist! twist! twist!
SO I HOPE YOU DON'T TAKE THIS PERSONALLY...
PPHHTT!
!
shunk!
WOT?
THUNK

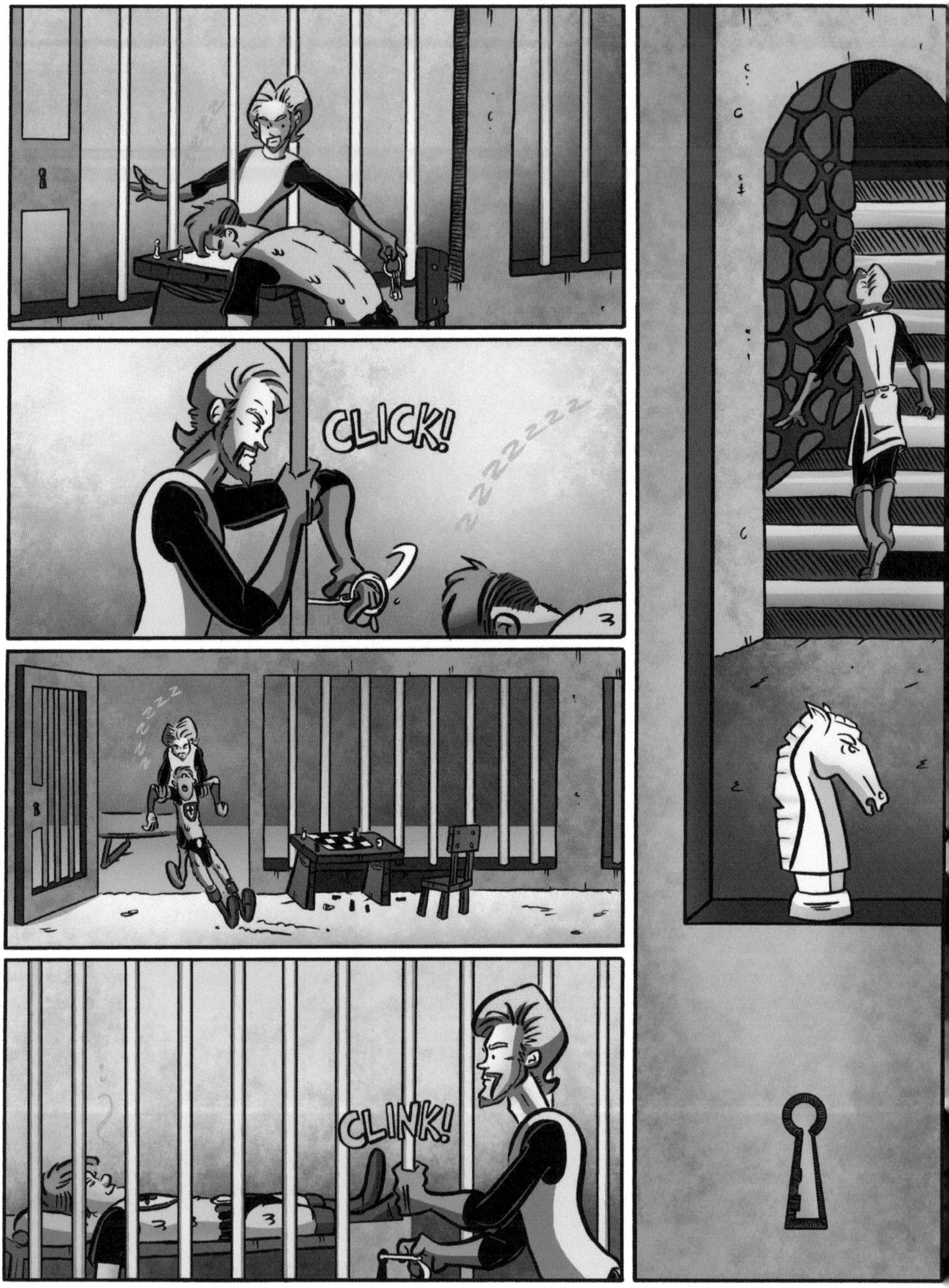
CLICK!
CLINK!

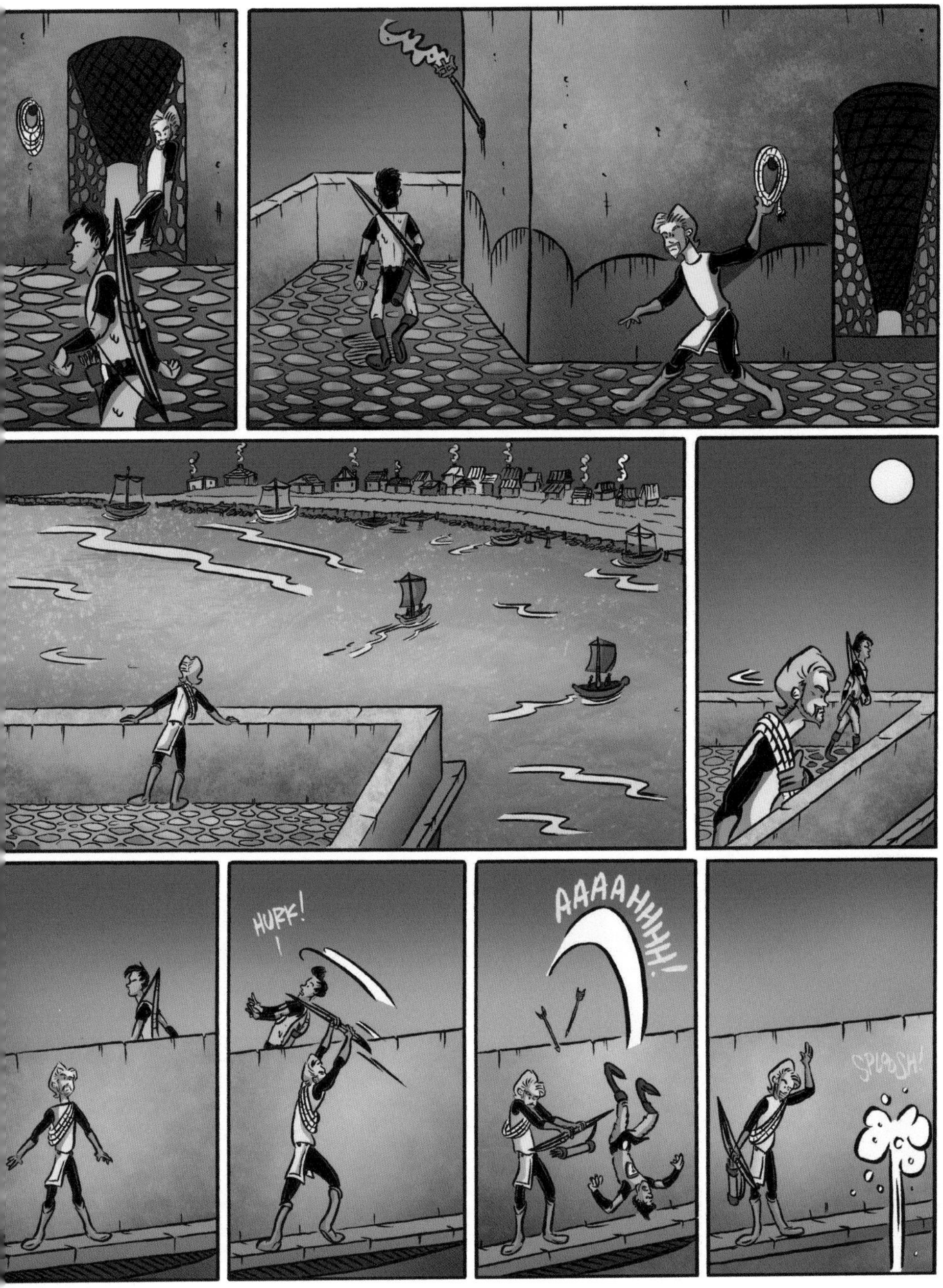
HURK!
AAAAHHHHH!
SPLOOSH!

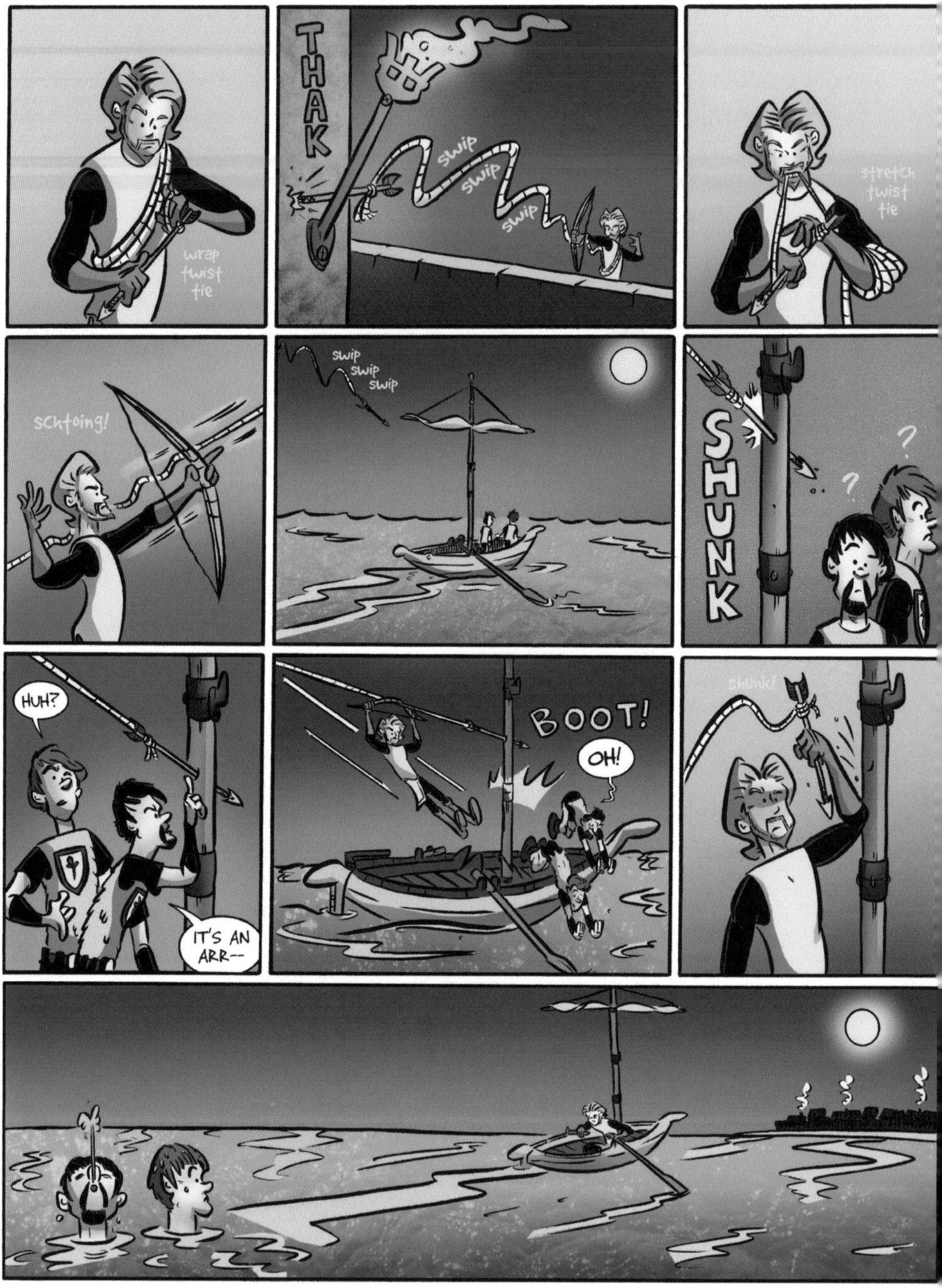
wrap
twist
tie
THAK
swip
swip
swip
stretch
twist
tie
schtoing!
swip
swip
swip
SHUNK
?
?
HUH?
IT'S AN
ARR--
BOOT!
OH!
shunk!

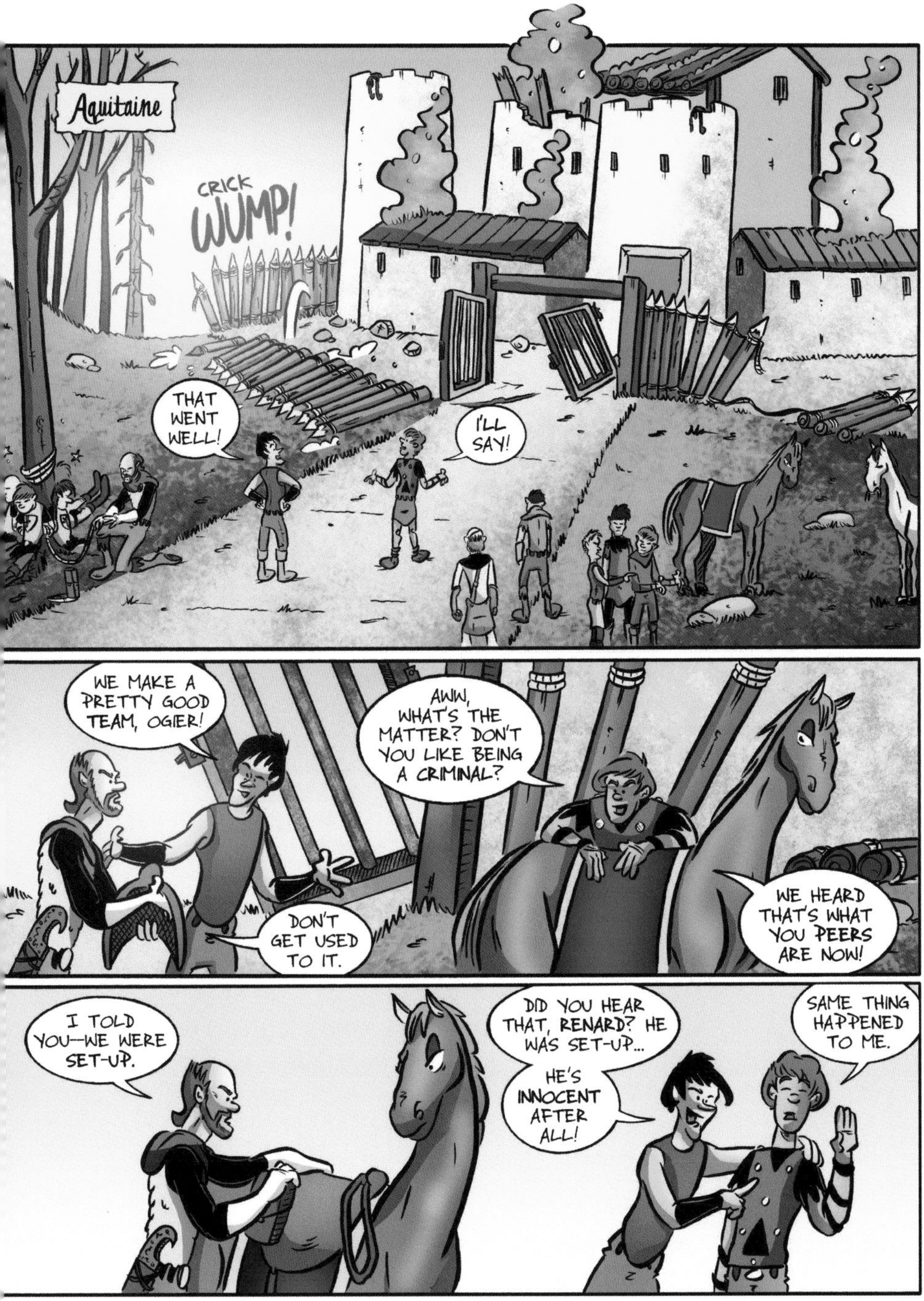
Aquitaine
CRICK
WUMP!
THAT WENT WELL!
I'LL SAY!
WE MAKE A PRETTY GOOD TEAM, OGIER!
DON'T GET USED TO IT.
AWW, WHAT'S THE MATTER? DON'T YOU LIKE BEING A CRIMINAL?
WE HEARD THAT'S WHAT YOU PEERS ARE NOW!
I TOLD YOU--WE WERE SET-UP.
DID YOU HEAR THAT, RENARD? HE WAS SET-UP...
HE'S INNOCENT AFTER ALL!
SAME THING HAPPENED TO ME.

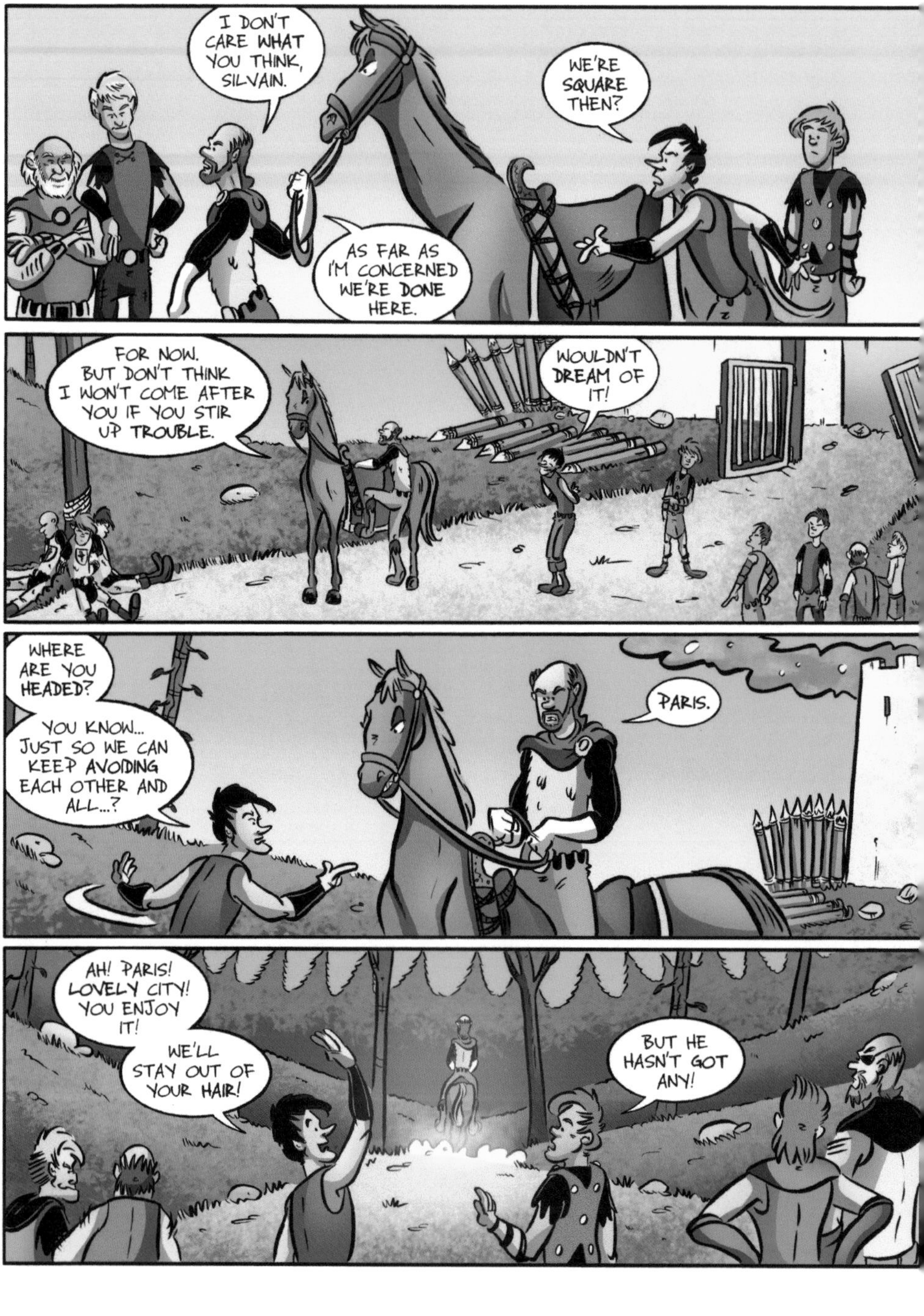
I DON'T CARE WHAT YOU THINK, SILVAIN.
WE'RE SQUARE THEN?
AS FAR AS I'M CONCERNED WE'RE DONE HERE.
FOR NOW. BUT DON'T THINK I WON'T COME AFTER YOU IF YOU STIR UP TROUBLE.
WOULDN'T DREAM OF IT!
WHERE ARE YOU HEADED?
YOU KNOW... JUST SO WE CAN KEEP AVOIDING EACH OTHER AND ALL...?
PARIS.
AH! PARIS! LOVELY CITY! YOU ENJOY IT!
WE'LL STAY OUT OF YOUR HAIR!
BUT HE HASN'T GOT ANY!

paladins tale

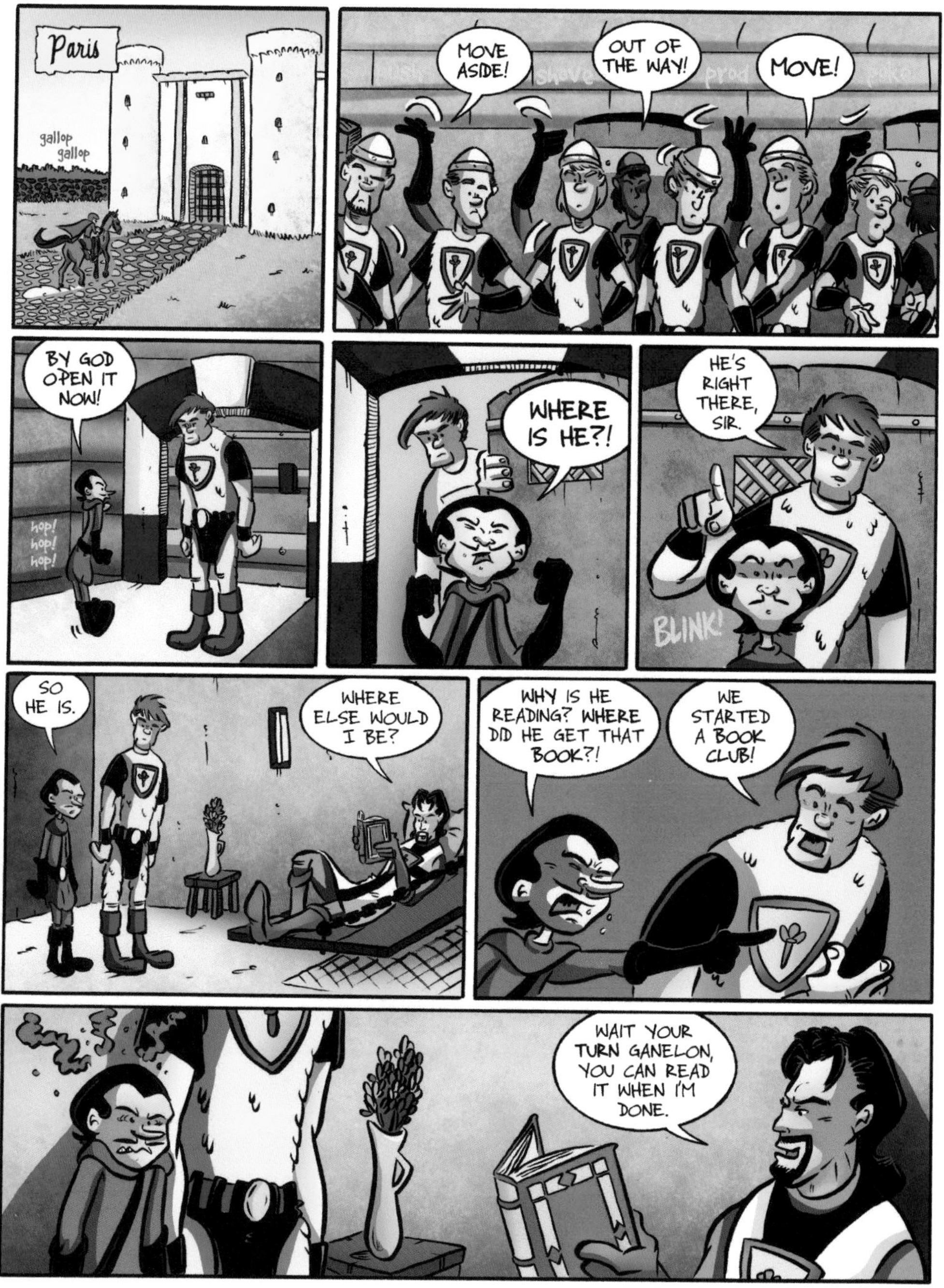

Paris
gallop gallop
MOVE ASIDE!
OUT OF THE WAY!
MOVE!
push shove prod poke
BY GOD OPEN IT NOW!
hop! hop! hop!
WHERE IS HE?!
HE'S RIGHT THERE, SIR.
BLINK!
SO HE IS.
WHERE ELSE WOULD I BE?
WHY IS HE READING? WHERE DID HE GET THAT BOOK?!
WE STARTED A BOOK CLUB!
WAIT YOUR TURN GANELON, YOU CAN READ IT WHEN I'M DONE.

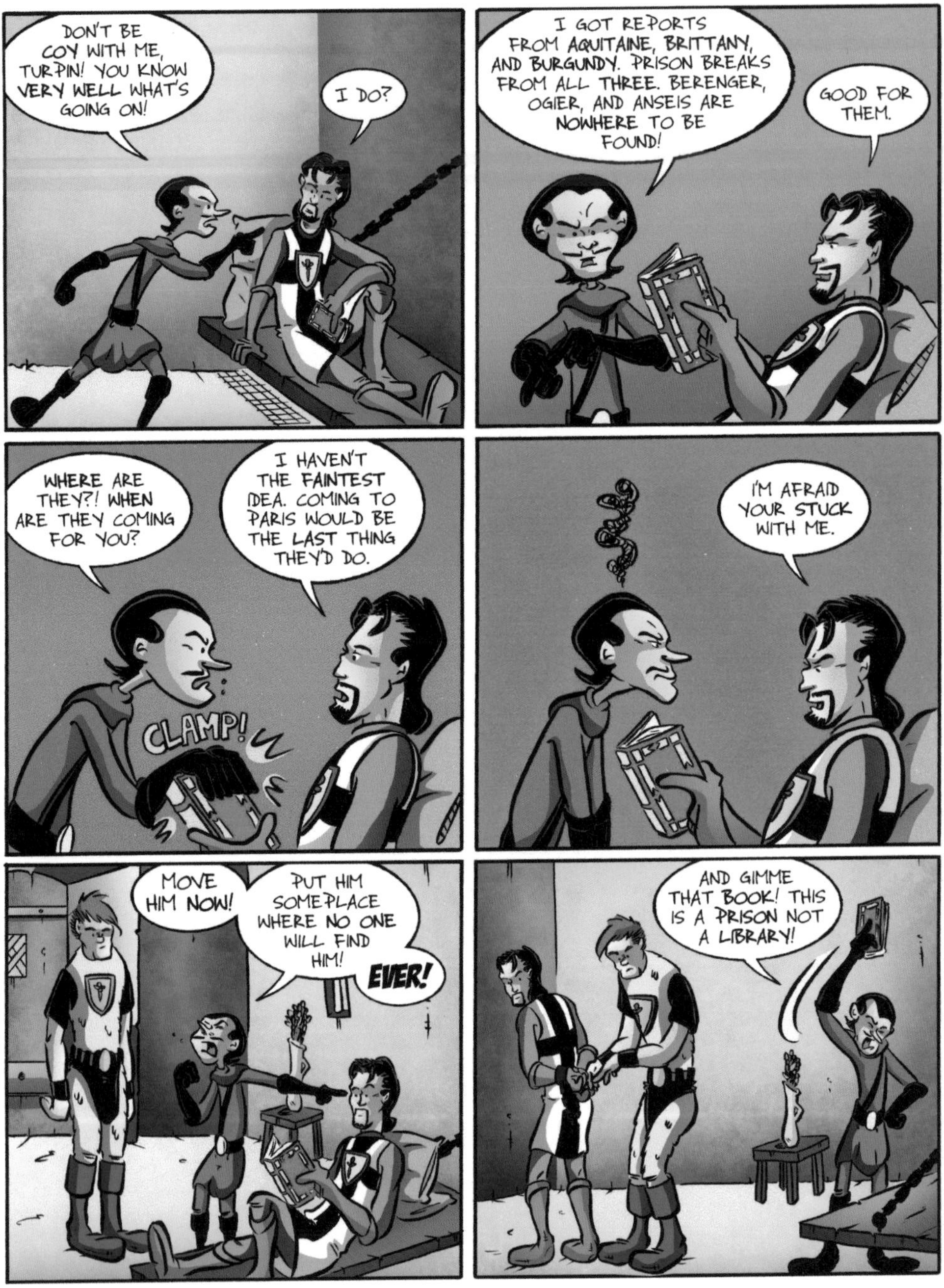
DON'T BE COY WITH ME, TURPIN! YOU KNOW VERY WELL WHAT'S GOING ON!
I DO?
I GOT REPORTS FROM AQUITAINE, BRITTANY, AND BURGUNDY. PRISON BREAKS FROM ALL THREE. BERENGER, OGIER, AND ANSEIS ARE NOWHERE TO BE FOUND!
GOOD FOR THEM.
WHERE ARE THEY?! WHEN ARE THEY COMING FOR YOU?
I HAVEN'T THE FAINTEST IDEA. COMING TO PARIS WOULD BE THE LAST THING THEY'D DO.
CLAMP!
I'M AFRAID YOUR STUCK WITH ME.
MOVE HIM NOW!
PUT HIM SOMEPLACE WHERE NO ONE WILL FIND HIM!
EVER!
AND GIMME THAT BOOK! THIS IS A PRISON NOT A LIBRARY!

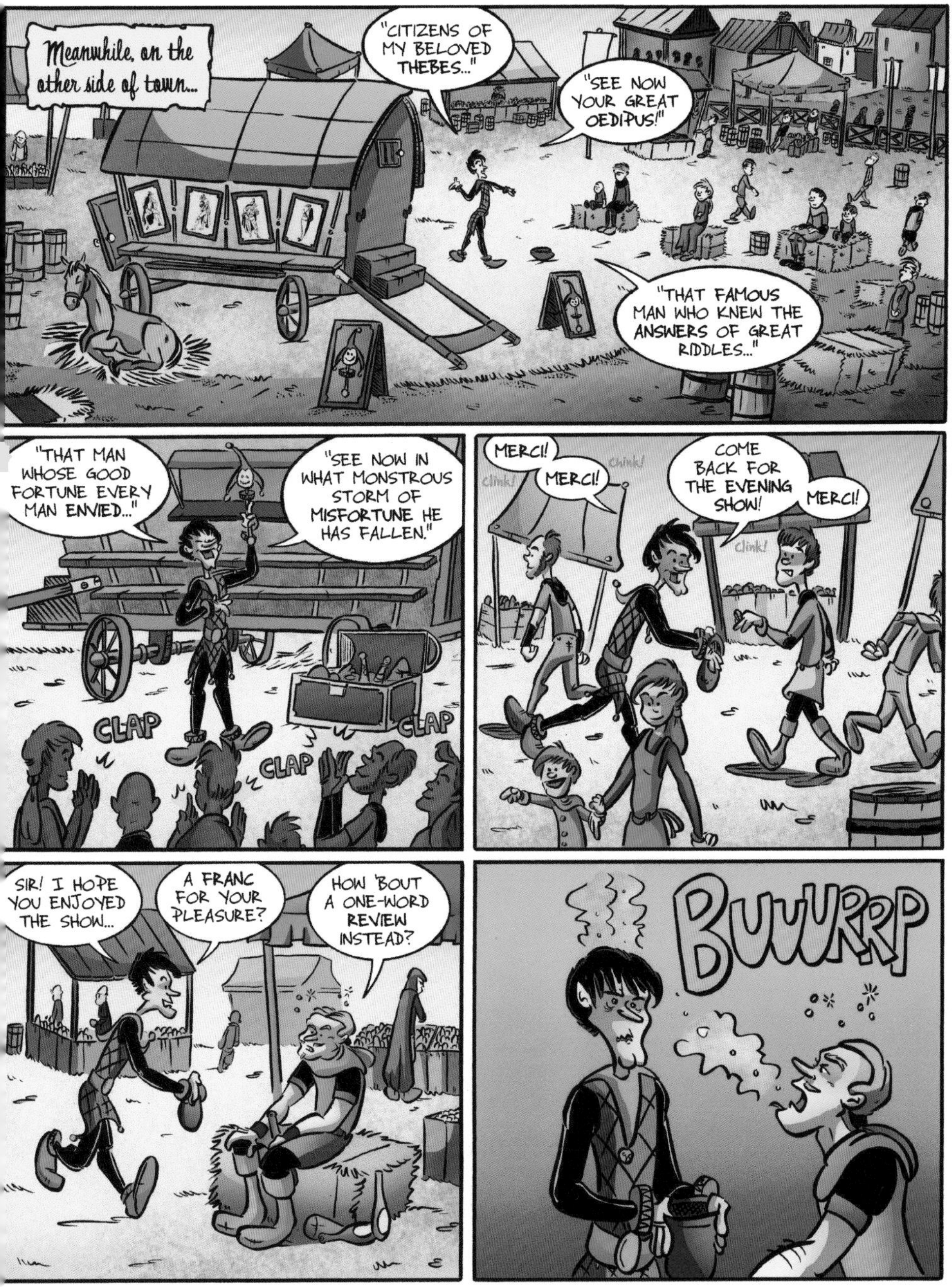

Meanwhile, on the other side of town...
"CITIZENS OF MY BELOVED THEBES..."
"SEE NOW YOUR GREAT OEDIPUS!"
"THAT FAMOUS MAN WHO KNEW THE ANSWERS OF GREAT RIDDLES..."
"THAT MAN WHOSE GOOD FORTUNE EVERY MAN ENVIED..."
"SEE NOW IN WHAT MONSTROUS STORM OF MISFORTUNE HE HAS FALLEN."
CLAP
CLAP
CLAP
MERCI!
Clink!
MERCI!
Clink!
COME BACK FOR THE EVENING SHOW!
MERCI!
Clink!
SIR! I HOPE YOU ENJOYED THE SHOW...
A FRANC FOR YOUR PLEASURE?
HOW 'BOUT A ONE-WORD REVIEW INSTEAD?
BUUURRP

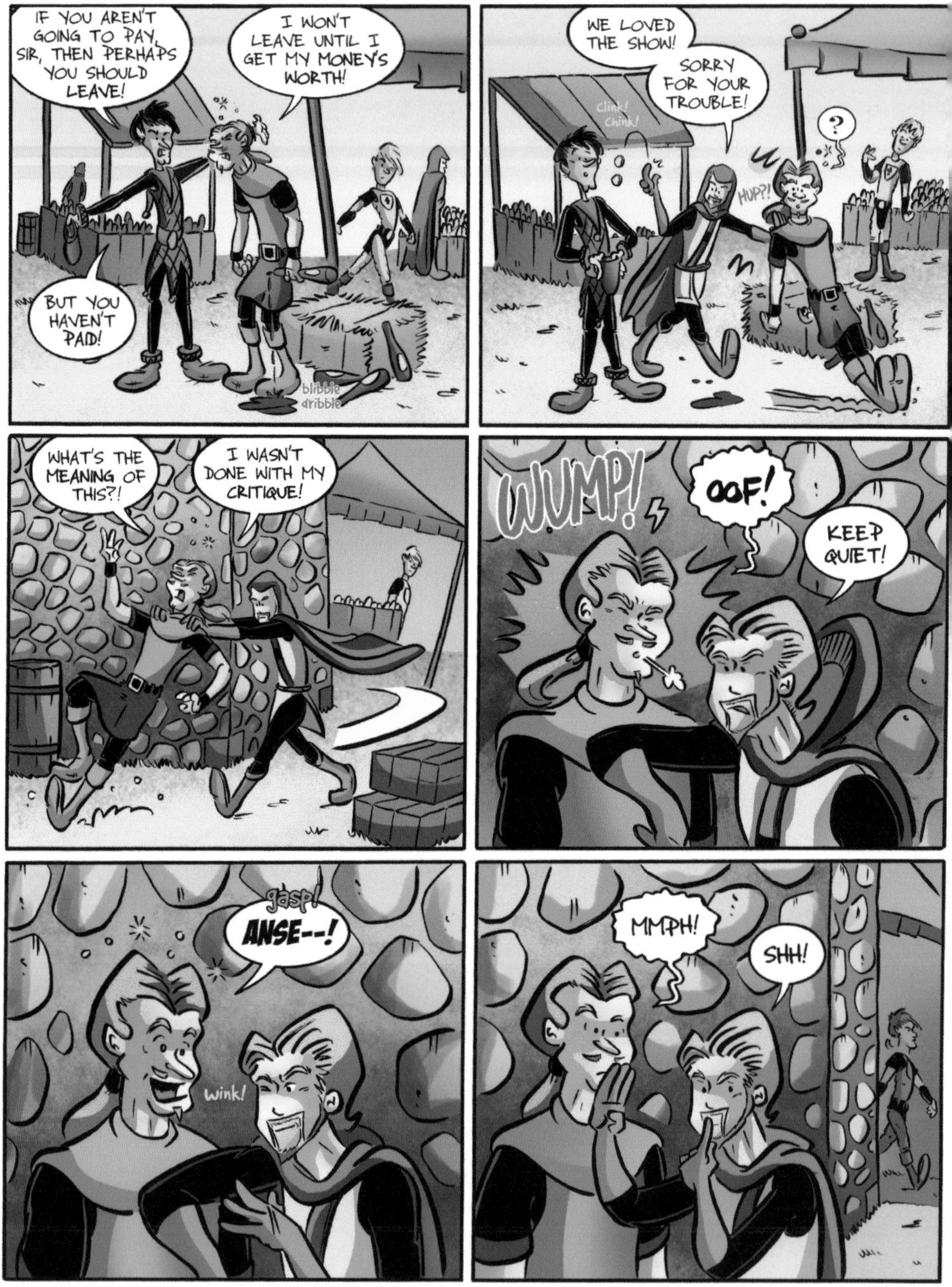
IF YOU AREN'T GOING TO PAY, SIR, THEN PERHAPS YOU SHOULD LEAVE!
I WON'T LEAVE UNTIL I GET MY MONEY'S WORTH!
BUT YOU HAVEN'T PAID!
blibble dribble
WE LOVED THE SHOW!
SORRY FOR YOUR TROUBLE!
Clink! Chink!
HUP?!
?
WHAT'S THE MEANING OF THIS?!
I WASN'T DONE WITH MY CRITIQUE!
WUMP!
OOF!
KEEP QUIET!
gasp!
ANSE--!
wink!
MMPH!
SHH!

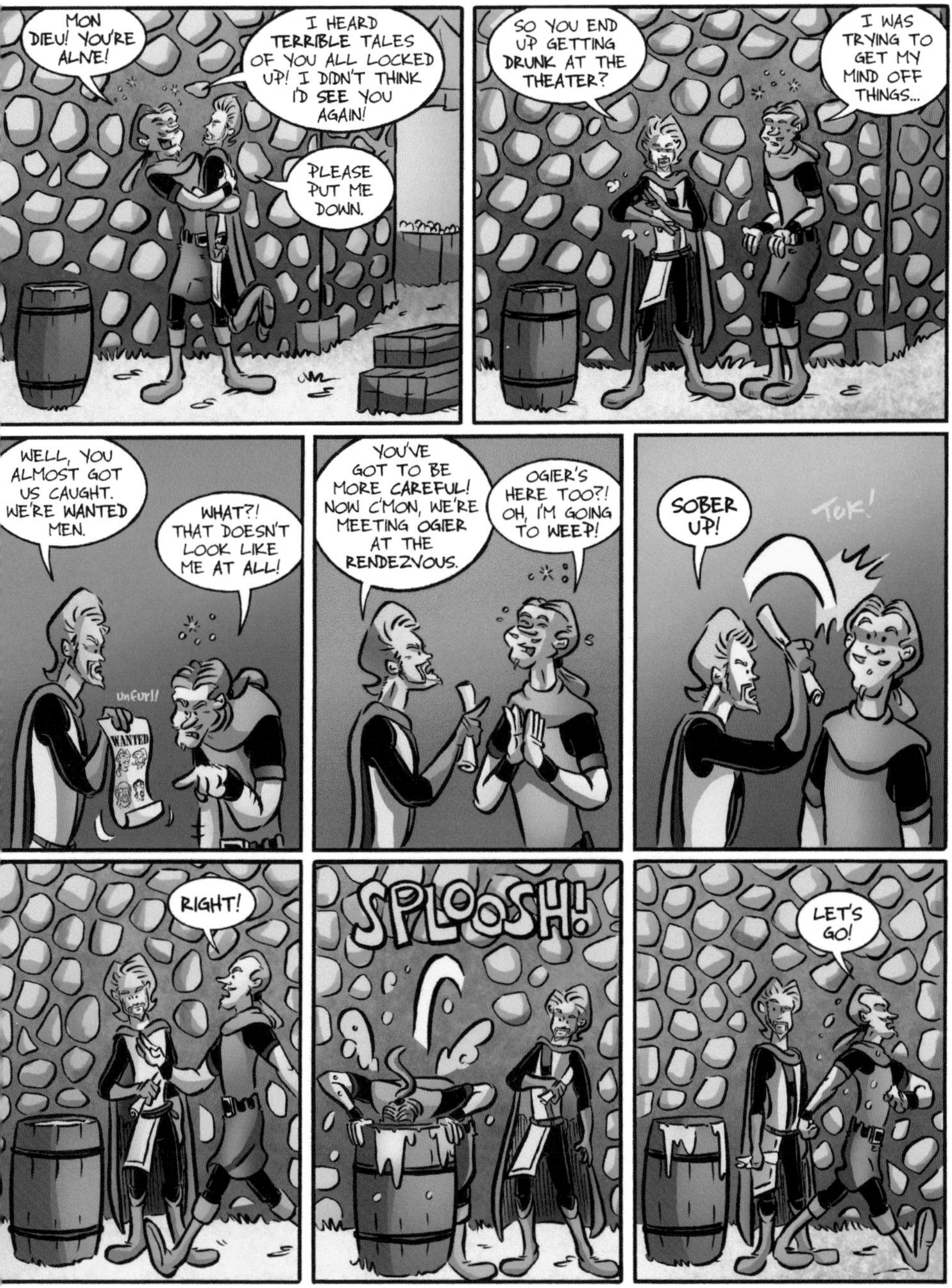
MON DIEU! YOU'RE ALIVE!
I HEARD TERRIBLE TALES OF YOU ALL LOCKED UP! I DIDN'T THINK I'D SEE YOU AGAIN!
PLEASE PUT ME DOWN.
SO YOU END UP GETTING DRUNK AT THE THEATER?
I WAS TRYING TO GET MY MIND OFF THINGS...
WELL, YOU ALMOST GOT US CAUGHT. WE'RE WANTED MEN.
WHAT?! THAT DOESN'T LOOK LIKE ME AT ALL!
unfurl!
WANTED
YOU'VE GOT TO BE MORE CAREFUL! NOW C'MON, WE'RE MEETING OGIER AT THE RENDEZVOUS.
OGIER'S HERE TOO?! OH, I'M GOING TO WEEP!
SOBER UP!
TOK!
RIGHT!
SPLOOSH!
LET'S GO!

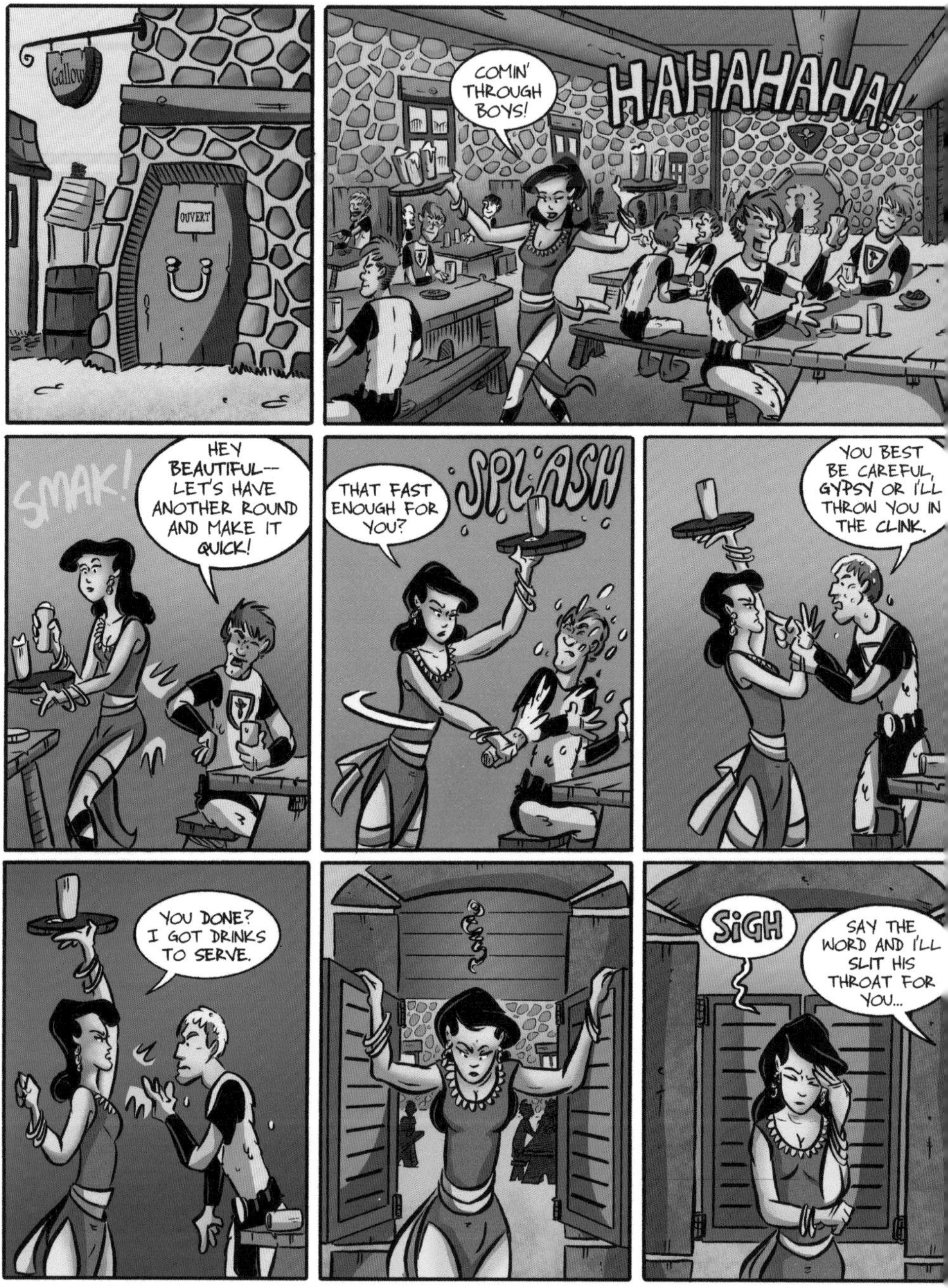
Gallows
OUVERT
COMIN' THROUGH BOYS!
HAHAHAHA!
SMAK!
HEY BEAUTIFUL-- LET'S HAVE ANOTHER ROUND AND MAKE IT QUICK!
THAT FAST ENOUGH FOR YOU?
SPLASH
YOU BEST BE CAREFUL, GYPSY OR I'LL THROW YOU IN THE CLINK.
YOU DONE? I GOT DRINKS TO SERVE.
SIGH
SAY THE WORD AND I'LL SLIT HIS THROAT FOR YOU...

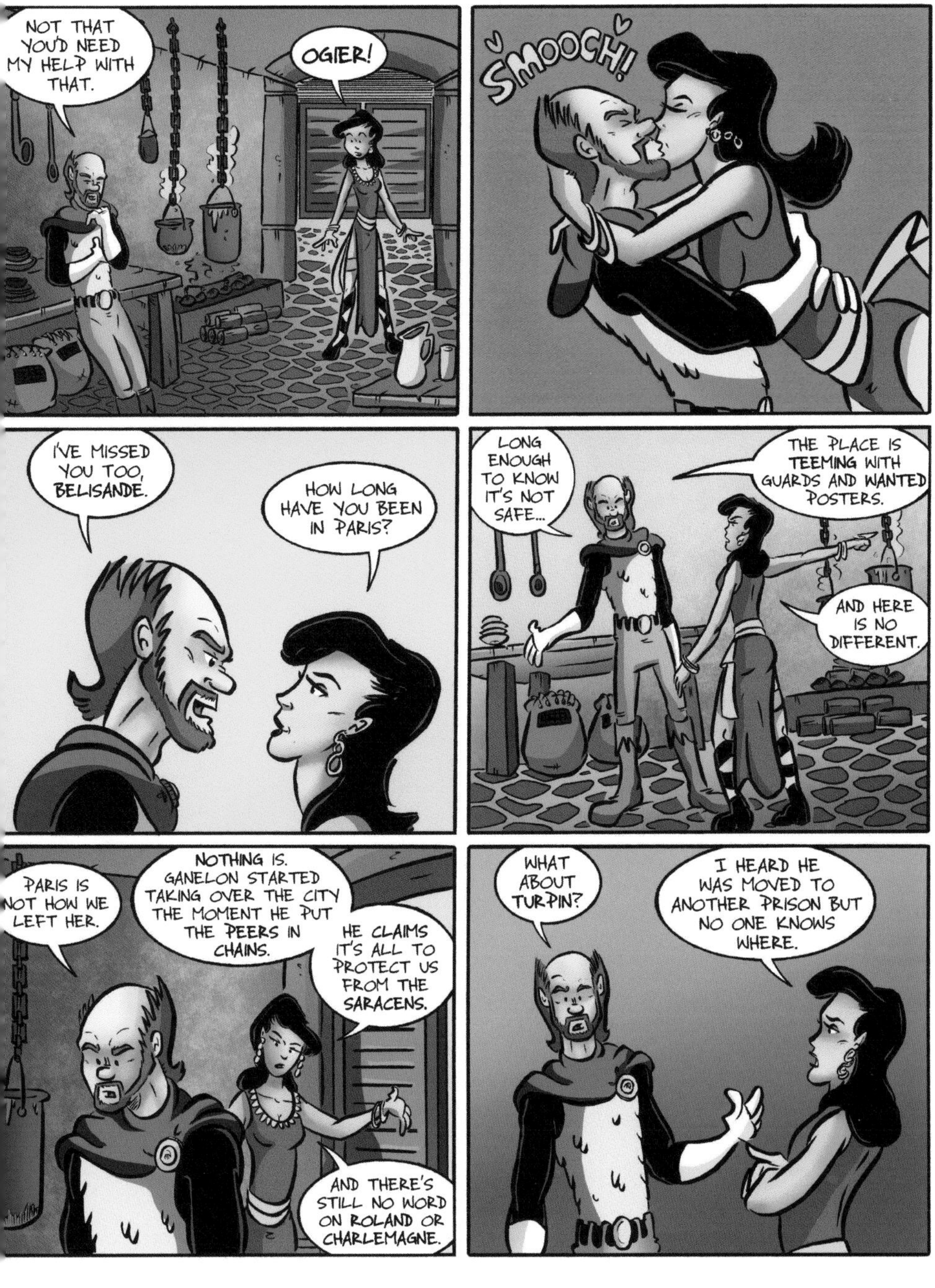
NOT THAT YOU'D NEED MY HELP WITH THAT.
OGIER!
SMOOCH!
I'VE MISSED YOU TOO, BELISANDE.
HOW LONG HAVE YOU BEEN IN PARIS?
LONG ENOUGH TO KNOW IT'S NOT SAFE...
THE PLACE IS TEEMING WITH GUARDS AND WANTED POSTERS.
AND HERE IS NO DIFFERENT.
PARIS IS NOT HOW WE LEFT HER.
NOTHING IS. GANELON STARTED TAKING OVER THE CITY THE MOMENT HE PUT THE PEERS IN CHAINS.
HE CLAIMS IT'S ALL TO PROTECT US FROM THE SARACENS.
AND THERE'S STILL NO WORD ON ROLAND OR CHARLEMAGNE.
WHAT ABOUT TURPIN?
I HEARD HE WAS MOVED TO ANOTHER PRISON BUT NO ONE KNOWS WHERE.

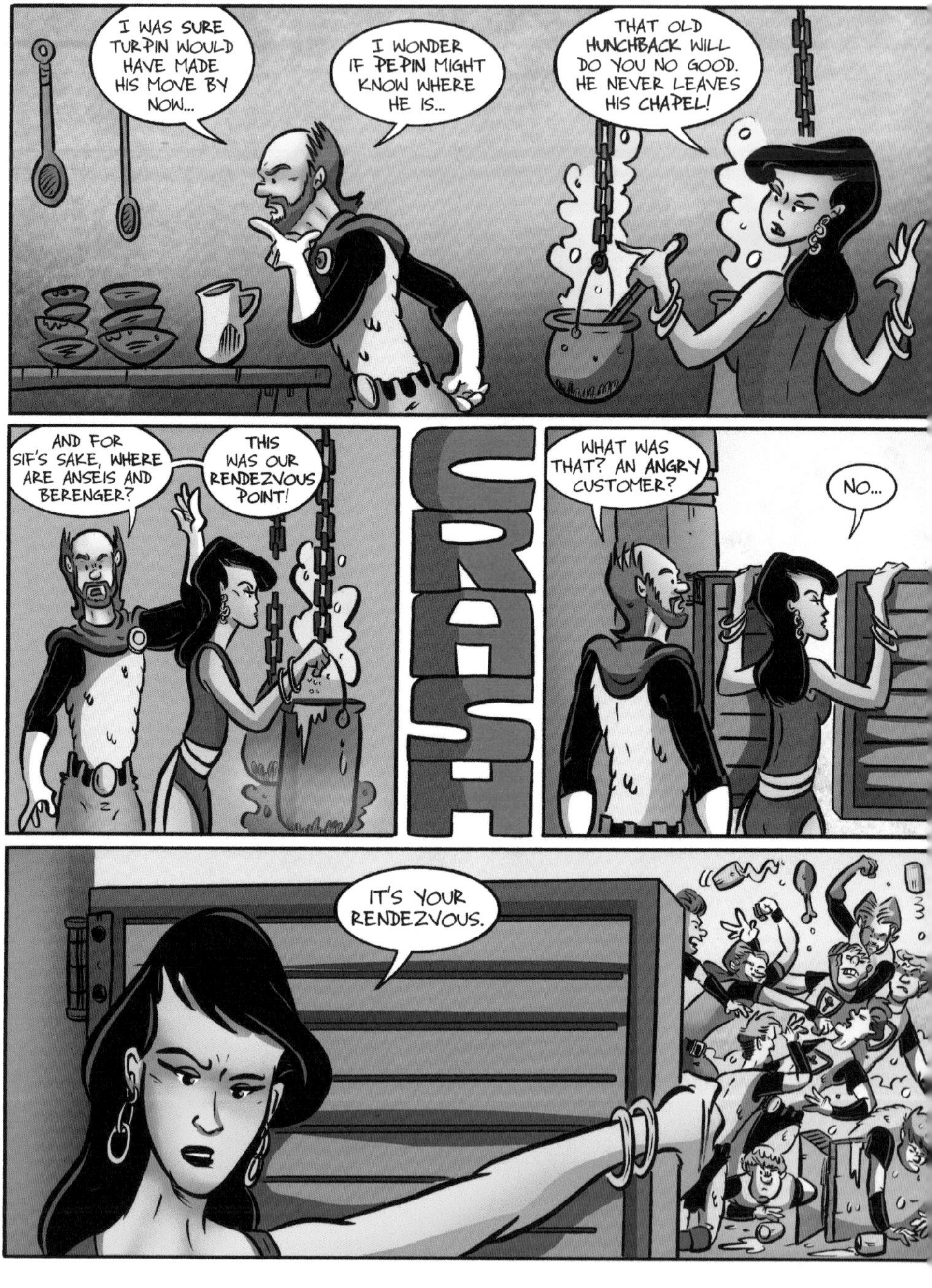
I WAS SURE TURPIN WOULD HAVE MADE HIS MOVE BY NOW...
I WONDER IF PEPIN MIGHT KNOW WHERE HE IS...
THAT OLD HUNCHBACK WILL DO YOU NO GOOD. HE NEVER LEAVES HIS CHAPEL!
AND FOR SIF'S SAKE, WHERE ARE ANSEIS AND BERENGER?
THIS WAS OUR RENDEZVOUS POINT!
CRASH
WHAT WAS THAT? AN ANGRY CUSTOMER?
NO...
IT'S YOUR RENDEZVOUS.

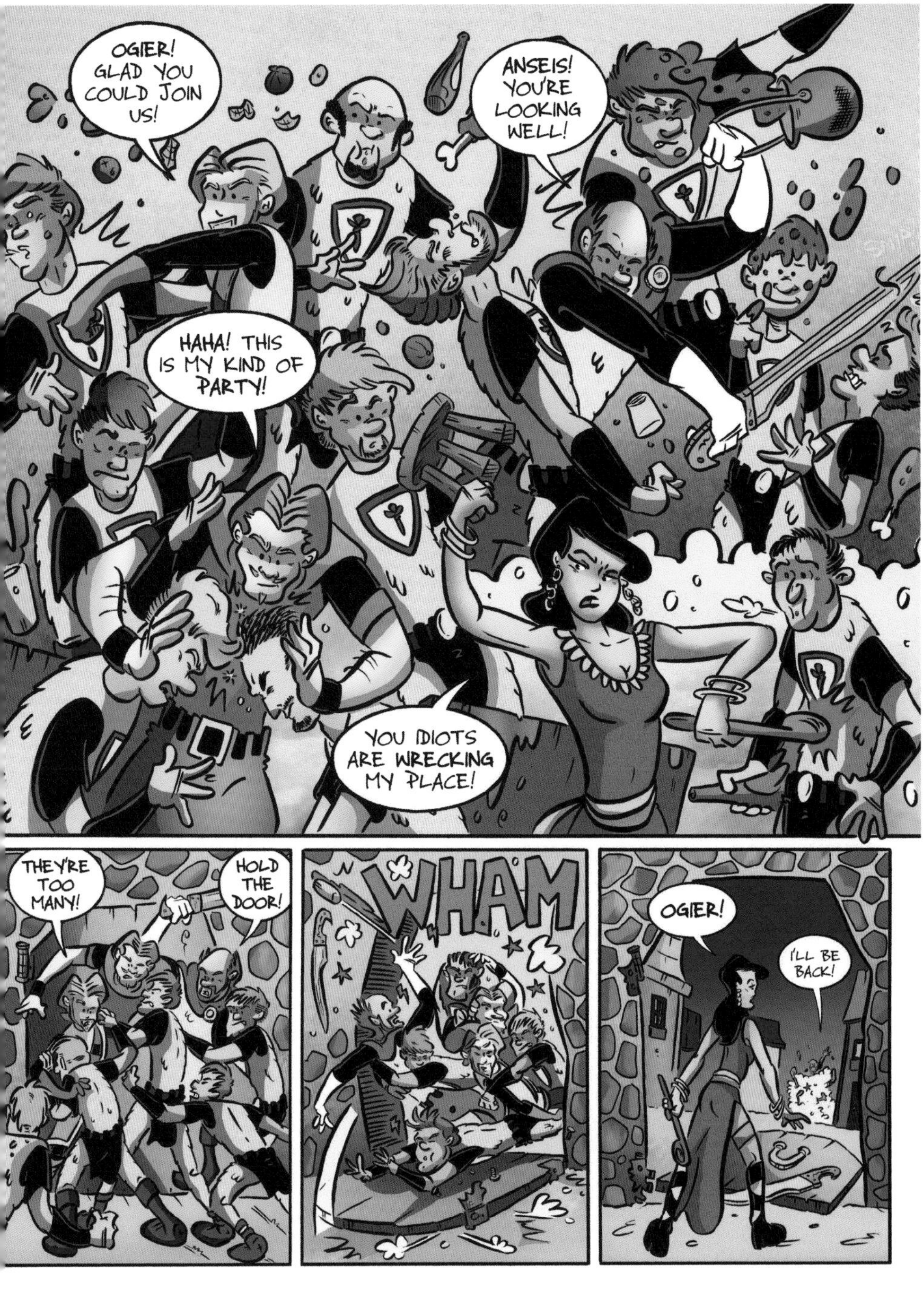
OGIER! GLAD YOU COULD JOIN US!
ANSEIS! YOU'RE LOOKING WELL!
HAHA! THIS IS MY KIND OF PARTY!
YOU IDIOTS ARE WRECKING MY PLACE!
THEY'RE TOO MANY!
HOLD THE DOOR!
WHAM
OGIER!
I'LL BE BACK!

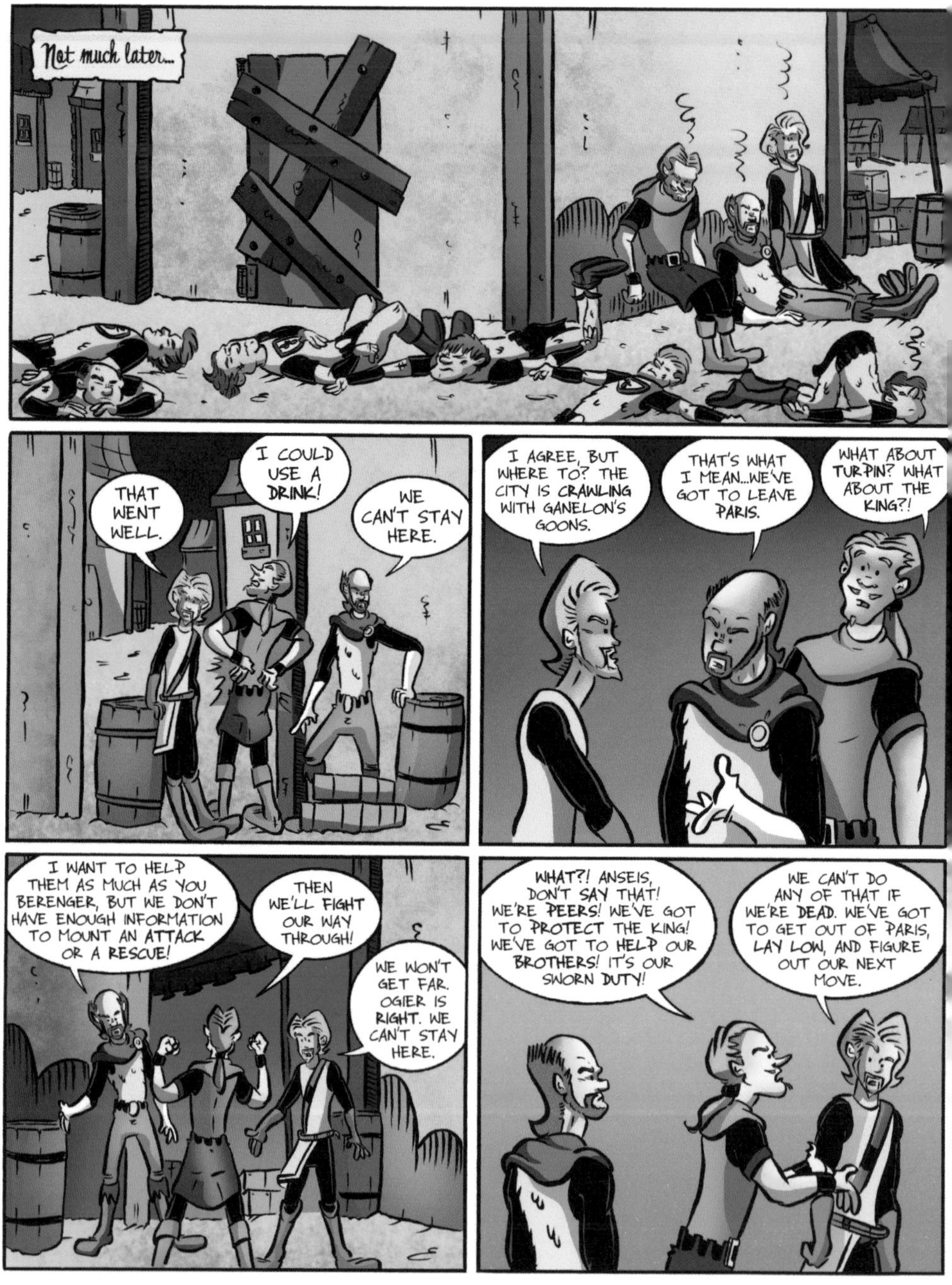
Not much later...
THAT WENT WELL.
I COULD USE A DRINK!
WE CAN'T STAY HERE.
I AGREE, BUT WHERE TO? THE CITY IS CRAWLING WITH GANELON'S GOONS.
THAT'S WHAT I MEAN...WE'VE GOT TO LEAVE PARIS.
WHAT ABOUT TURPIN? WHAT ABOUT THE KING?!
I WANT TO HELP THEM AS MUCH AS YOU BERENGER, BUT WE DON'T HAVE ENOUGH INFORMATION TO MOUNT AN ATTACK OR A RESCUE!
THEN WE'LL FIGHT OUR WAY THROUGH!
WE WON'T GET FAR. OGIER IS RIGHT. WE CAN'T STAY HERE.
WHAT?! ANSEIS, DON'T SAY THAT! WE'RE PEERS! WE'VE GOT TO PROTECT THE KING! WE'VE GOT TO HELP OUR BROTHERS! IT'S OUR SWORN DUTY!
WE CAN'T DO ANY OF THAT IF WE'RE DEAD. WE'VE GOT TO GET OUT OF PARIS, LAY LOW, AND FIGURE OUT OUR NEXT MOVE.

SO WHAT IS OUR NEXT MOVE?
I'M THINKING!
WELL THINK FASTER!
HMM...
QUIET YOU TWO!
I'VE GOT AN IDEA!
HOW EXACTLY IS THIS GOING TO WORK?
JUST SHUT-UP AND PUT THIS ON!
HEY! WHAT'S GOING ON HERE?

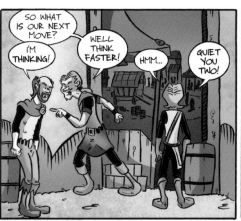

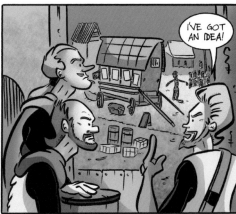

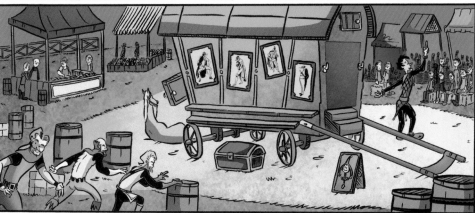

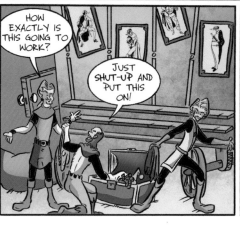

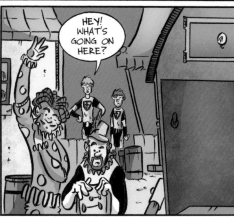

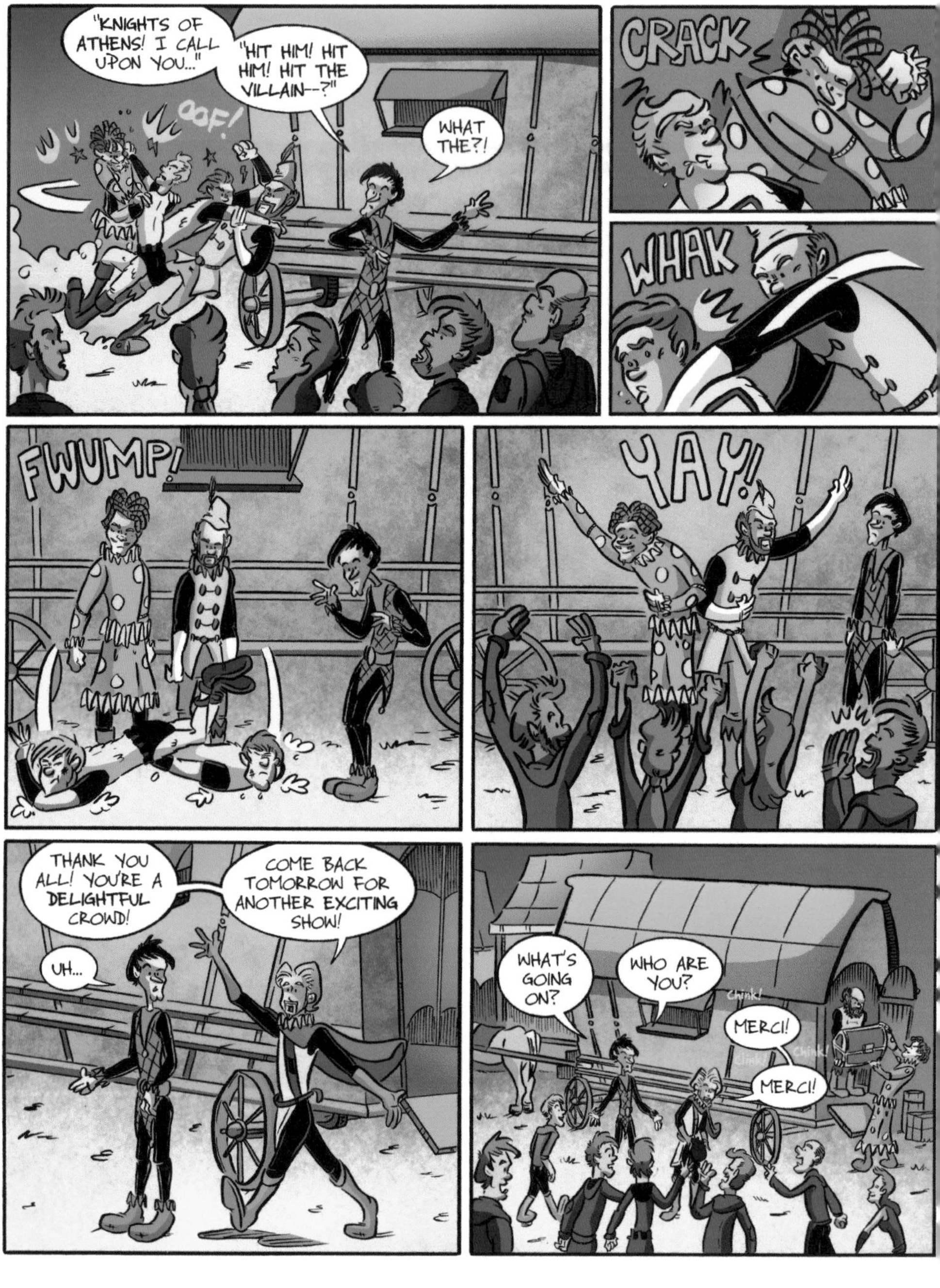
"KNIGHTS OF ATHENS! I CALL UPON YOU..."
"HIT HIM! HIT HIM! HIT THE VILLAIN--?"
OOF!
WHAT THE?!
CRACK
WHAK
FWUMP!
YAY!
THANK YOU ALL! YOU'RE A DELIGHTFUL CROWD!
COME BACK TOMORROW FOR ANOTHER EXCITING SHOW!
UH...
WHAT'S GOING ON?
WHO ARE YOU?
MERCI!
MERCI!

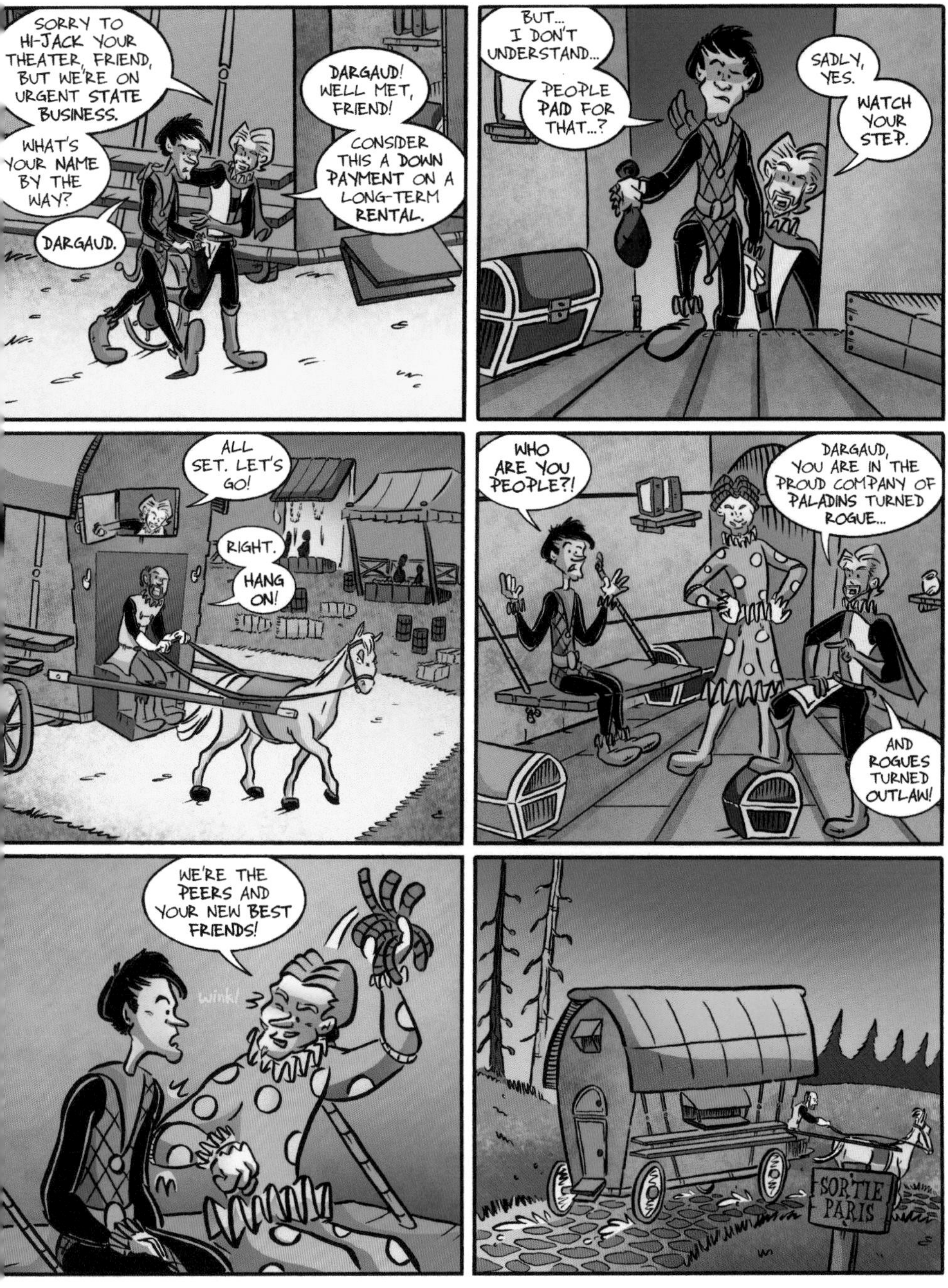
SORRY TO HI-JACK YOUR THEATER, FRIEND, BUT WE'RE ON URGENT STATE BUSINESS.
WHAT'S YOUR NAME BY THE WAY?
DARGAUD.
DARGAUD! WELL MET, FRIEND!
CONSIDER THIS A DOWN PAYMENT ON A LONG-TERM RENTAL.
BUT... I DON'T UNDERSTAND...
PEOPLE PAID FOR THAT...?
SADLY, YES.
WATCH YOUR STEP.
ALL SET. LET'S GO!
RIGHT.
HANG ON!
WHO ARE YOU PEOPLE?!
DARGAUD, YOU ARE IN THE PROUD COMPANY OF PALADINS TURNED ROGUE...
AND ROGUES TURNED OUTLAW!
WE'RE THE PEERS AND YOUR NEW BEST FRIENDS!
wink!
SORTIE PARIS

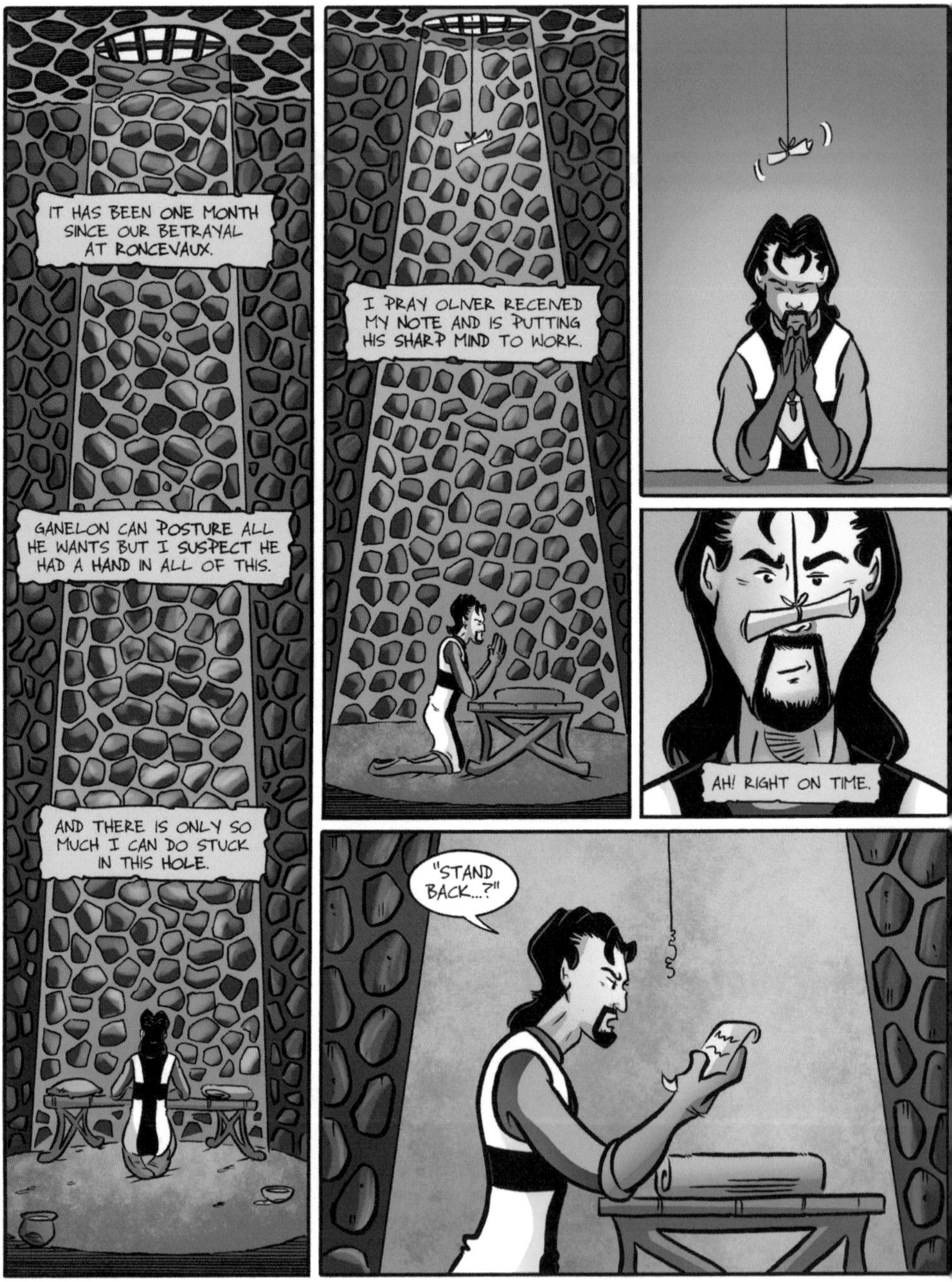
IT HAS BEEN ONE MONTH SINCE OUR BETRAYAL AT RONCEVAUX.
GANELON CAN POSTURE ALL HE WANTS BUT I SUSPECT HE HAD A HAND IN ALL OF THIS.
AND THERE IS ONLY SO MUCH I CAN DO STUCK IN THIS HOLE.
I PRAY OLIVER RECEIVED MY NOTE AND IS PUTTING HIS SHARP MIND TO WORK.
AH! RIGHT ON TIME.
"STAND BACK...?"

paladins tale

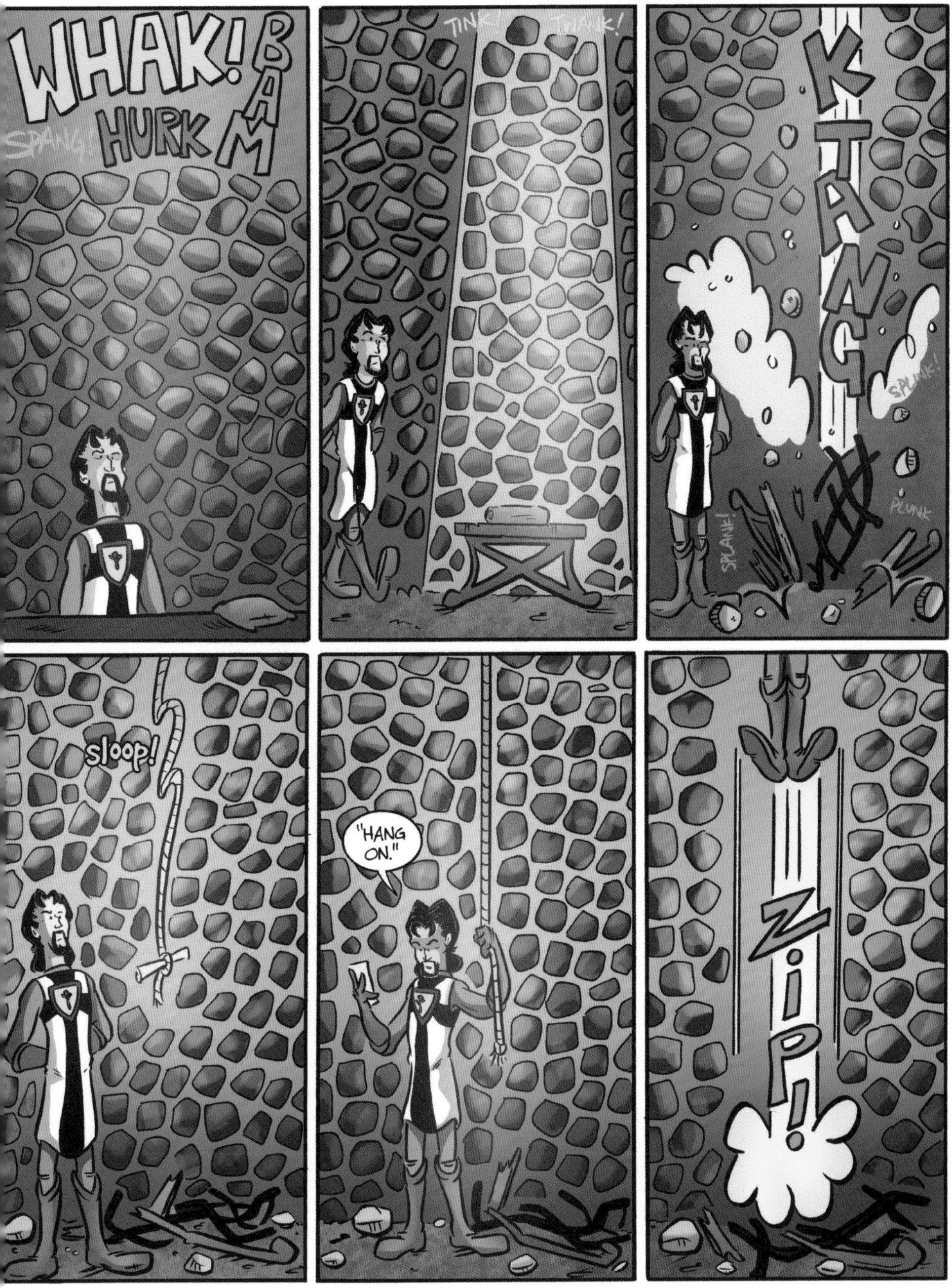
WHAK!
BAM
SPANG!
HURK
TINK!
TWANK!
KTANG
SPLUNK!
PLUNK
SPLANK!
sloop!
"HANG ON."
ZiP!

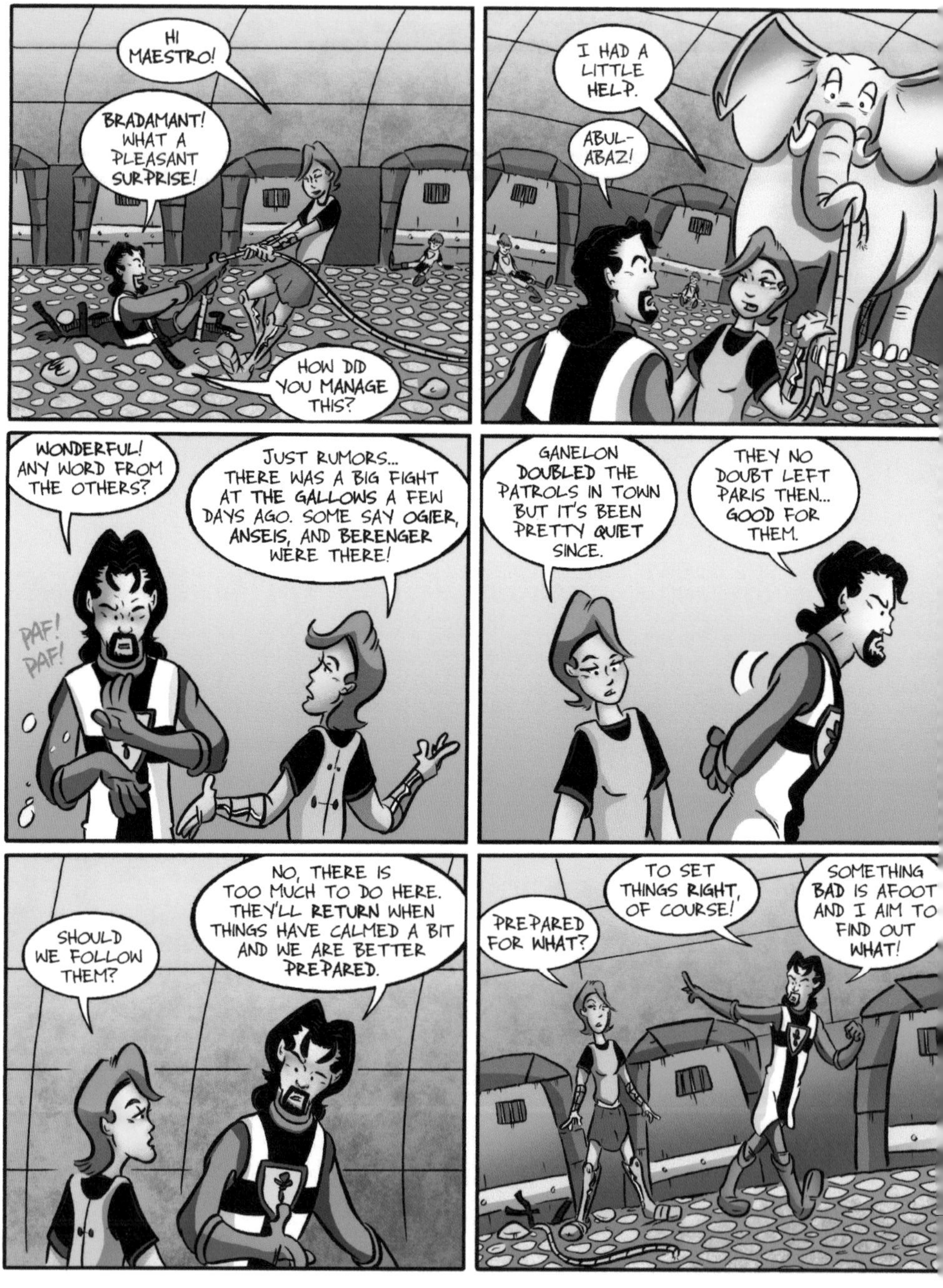
HI MAESTRO!
BRADAMANT! WHAT A PLEASANT SURPRISE!
HOW DID YOU MANAGE THIS?
I HAD A LITTLE HELP.
ABUL-ABAZ!
WONDERFUL! ANY WORD FROM THE OTHERS?
JUST RUMORS... THERE WAS A BIG FIGHT AT THE GALLOWS A FEW DAYS AGO. SOME SAY OGIER, ANSEIS, AND BERENGER WERE THERE!
PAF! PAF!
GANELON DOUBLED THE PATROLS IN TOWN BUT IT'S BEEN PRETTY QUIET SINCE.
THEY NO DOUBT LEFT PARIS THEN... GOOD FOR THEM.
SHOULD WE FOLLOW THEM?
NO, THERE IS TOO MUCH TO DO HERE. THEY'LL RETURN WHEN THINGS HAVE CALMED A BIT AND WE ARE BETTER PREPARED.
PREPARED FOR WHAT?
TO SET THINGS RIGHT, OF COURSE!
SOMETHING BAD IS AFOOT AND I AIM TO FIND OUT WHAT!

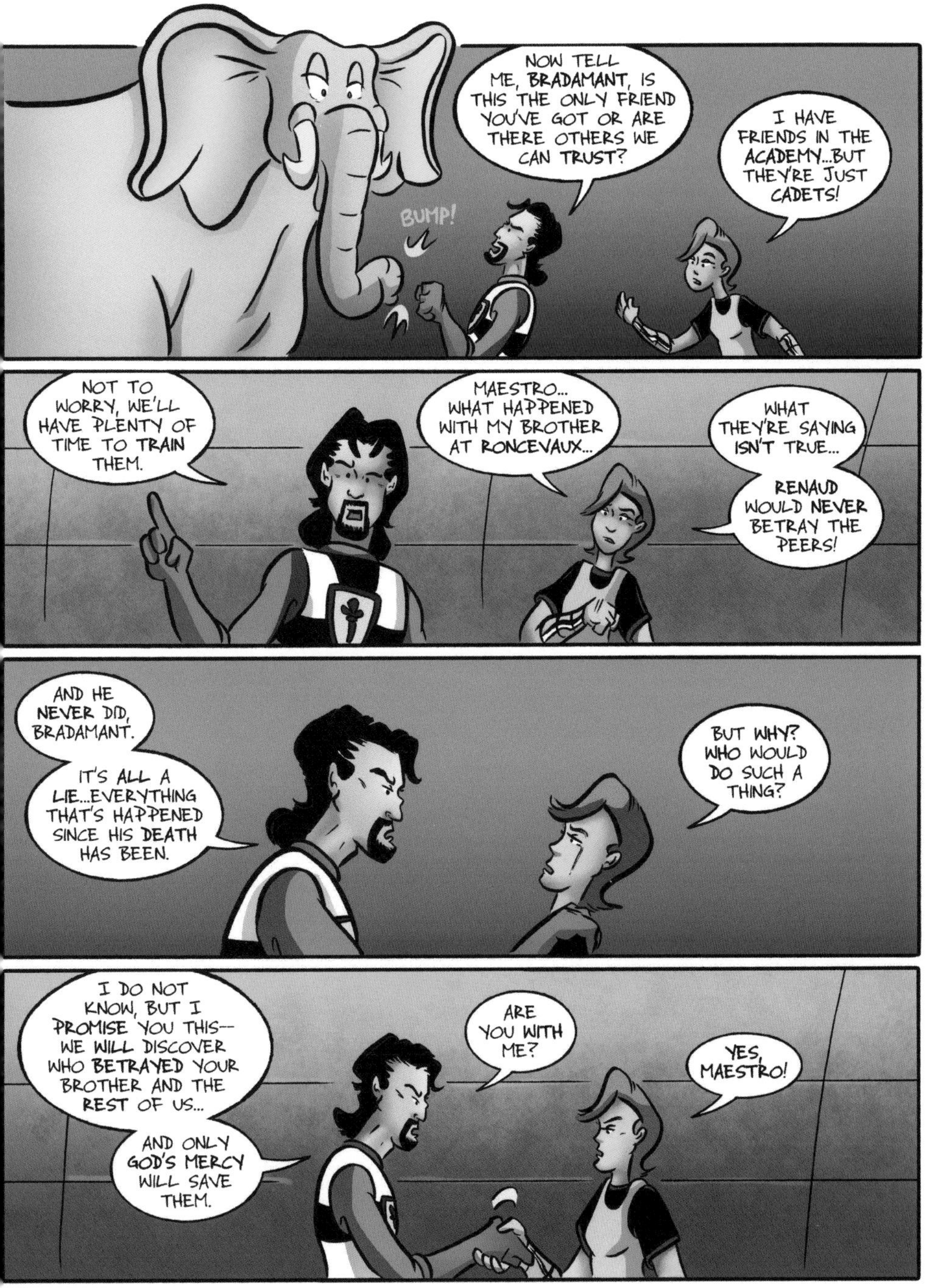
NOW TELL ME, BRADAMANT, IS THIS THE ONLY FRIEND YOU'VE GOT OR ARE THERE OTHERS WE CAN TRUST?
BUMP!
I HAVE FRIENDS IN THE ACADEMY...BUT THEY'RE JUST CADETS!
NOT TO WORRY, WE'LL HAVE PLENTY OF TIME TO TRAIN THEM.
MAESTRO... WHAT HAPPENED WITH MY BROTHER AT RONCEVAUX...
WHAT THEY'RE SAYING ISN'T TRUE...
RENAUD WOULD NEVER BETRAY THE PEERS!
AND HE NEVER DID, BRADAMANT.
IT'S ALL A LIE...EVERYTHING THAT'S HAPPENED SINCE HIS DEATH HAS BEEN.
BUT WHY? WHO WOULD DO SUCH A THING?
I DO NOT KNOW, BUT I PROMISE YOU THIS-- WE WILL DISCOVER WHO BETRAYED YOUR BROTHER AND THE REST OF US...
AND ONLY GOD'S MERCY WILL SAVE THEM.
ARE YOU WITH ME?
YES, MAESTRO!

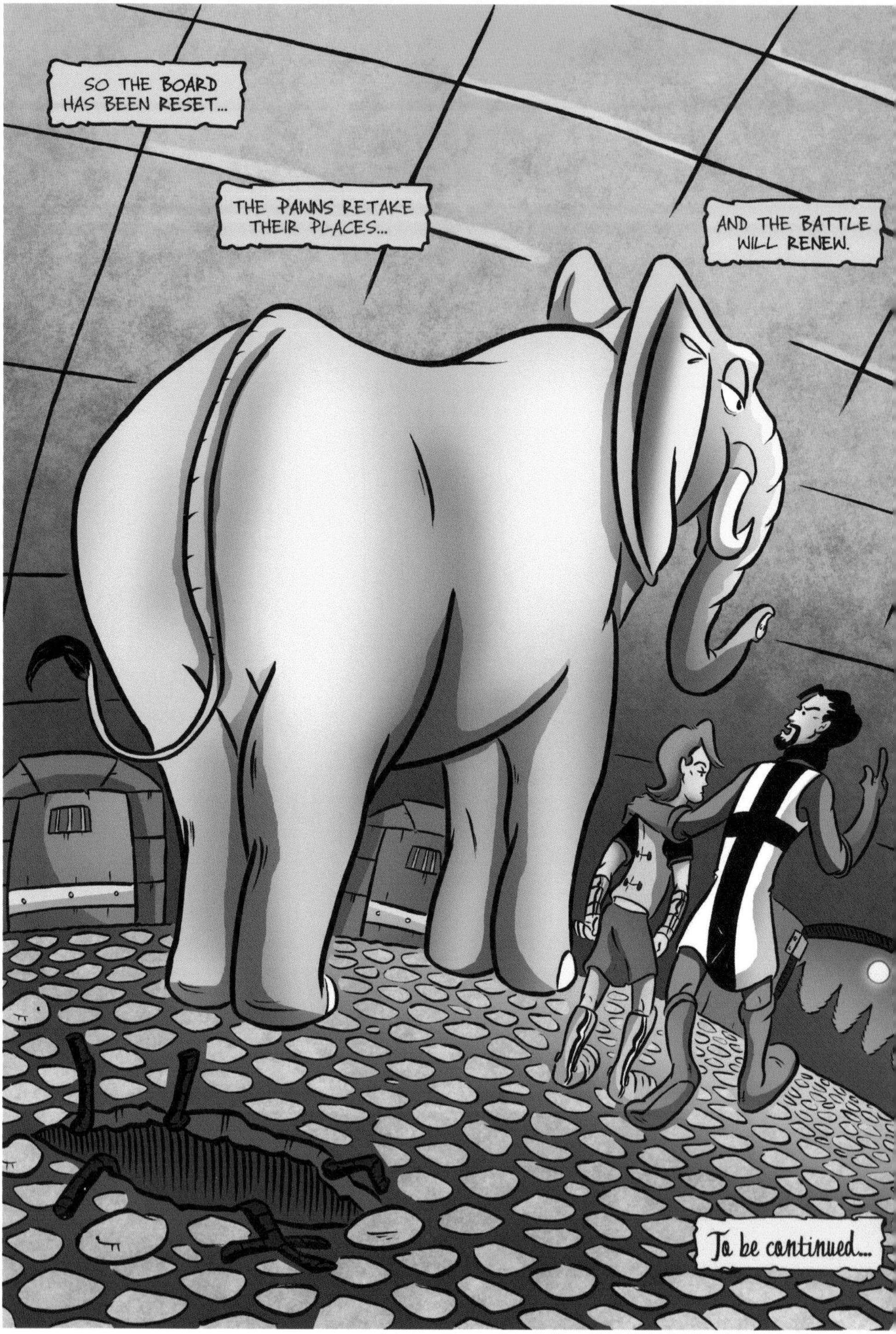
SO THE BOARD HAS BEEN RESET...
THE PAWNS RETAKE THEIR PLACES...
AND THE BATTLE WILL RENEW.
To be continued...

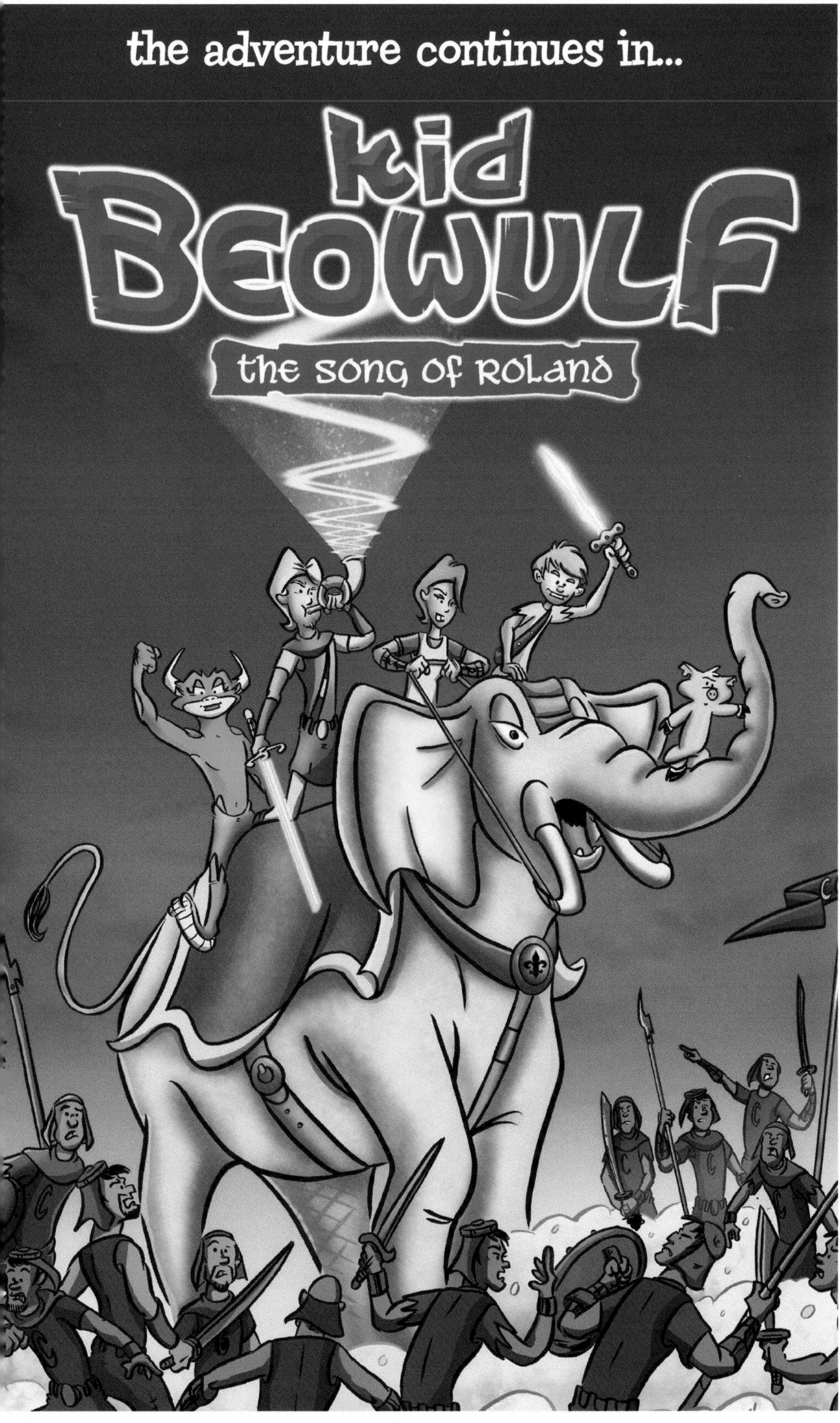
the adventure continues in...
kid Beowulf
the song of Roland

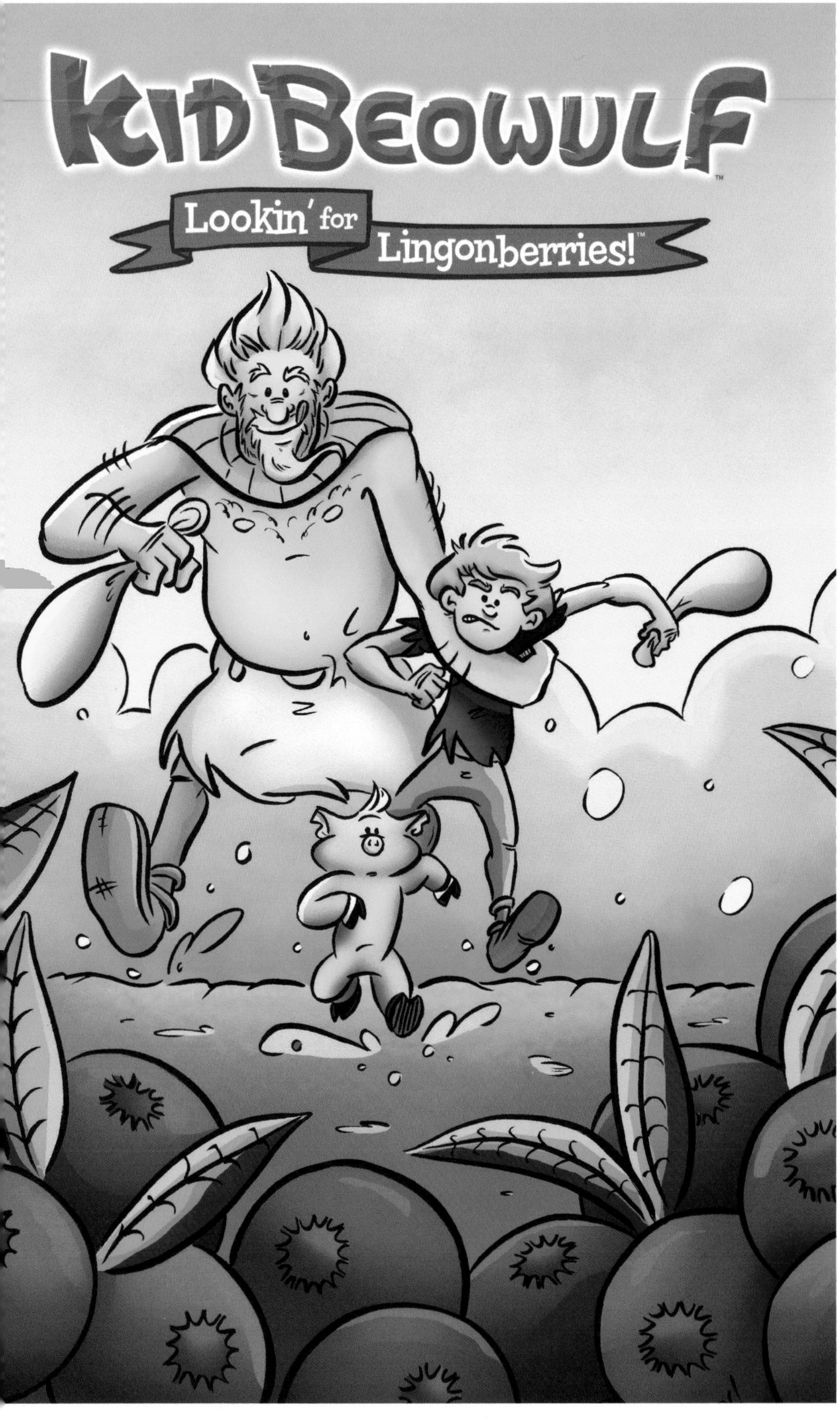

KID BEOWULF™
Lookin' for Lingonberries!™

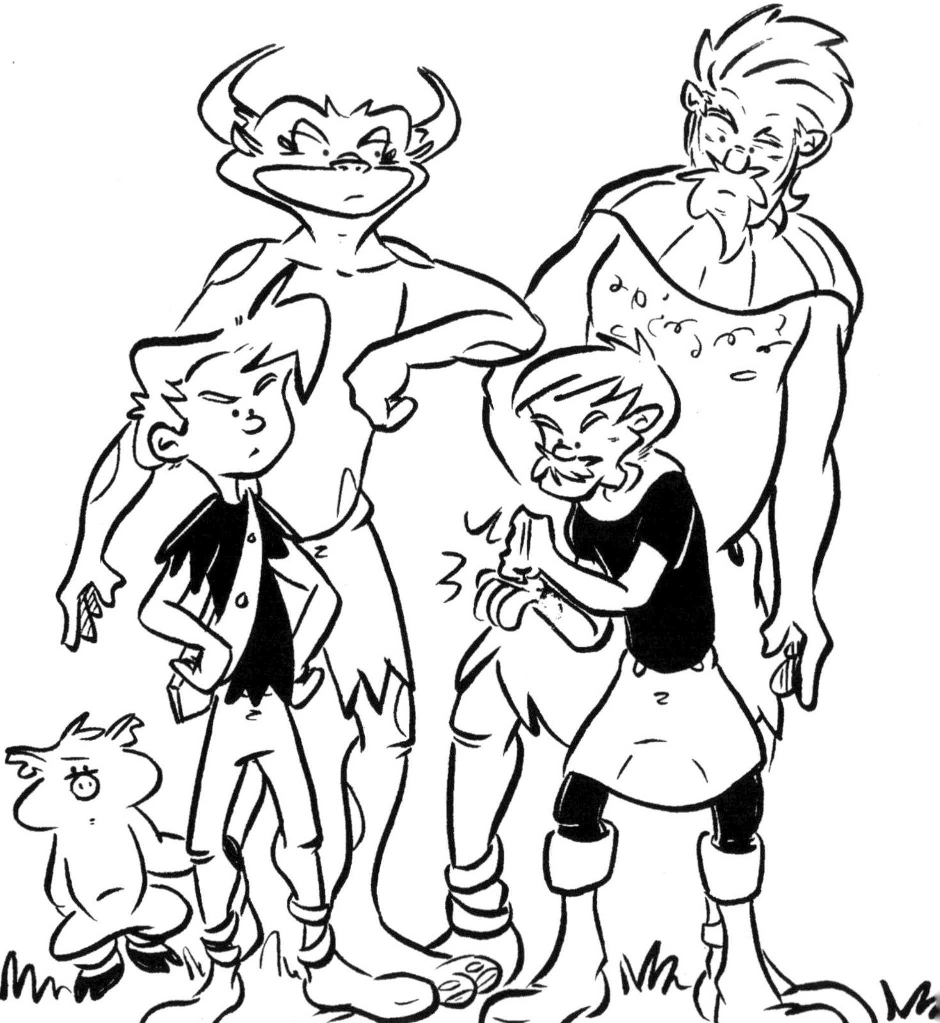
LEX!

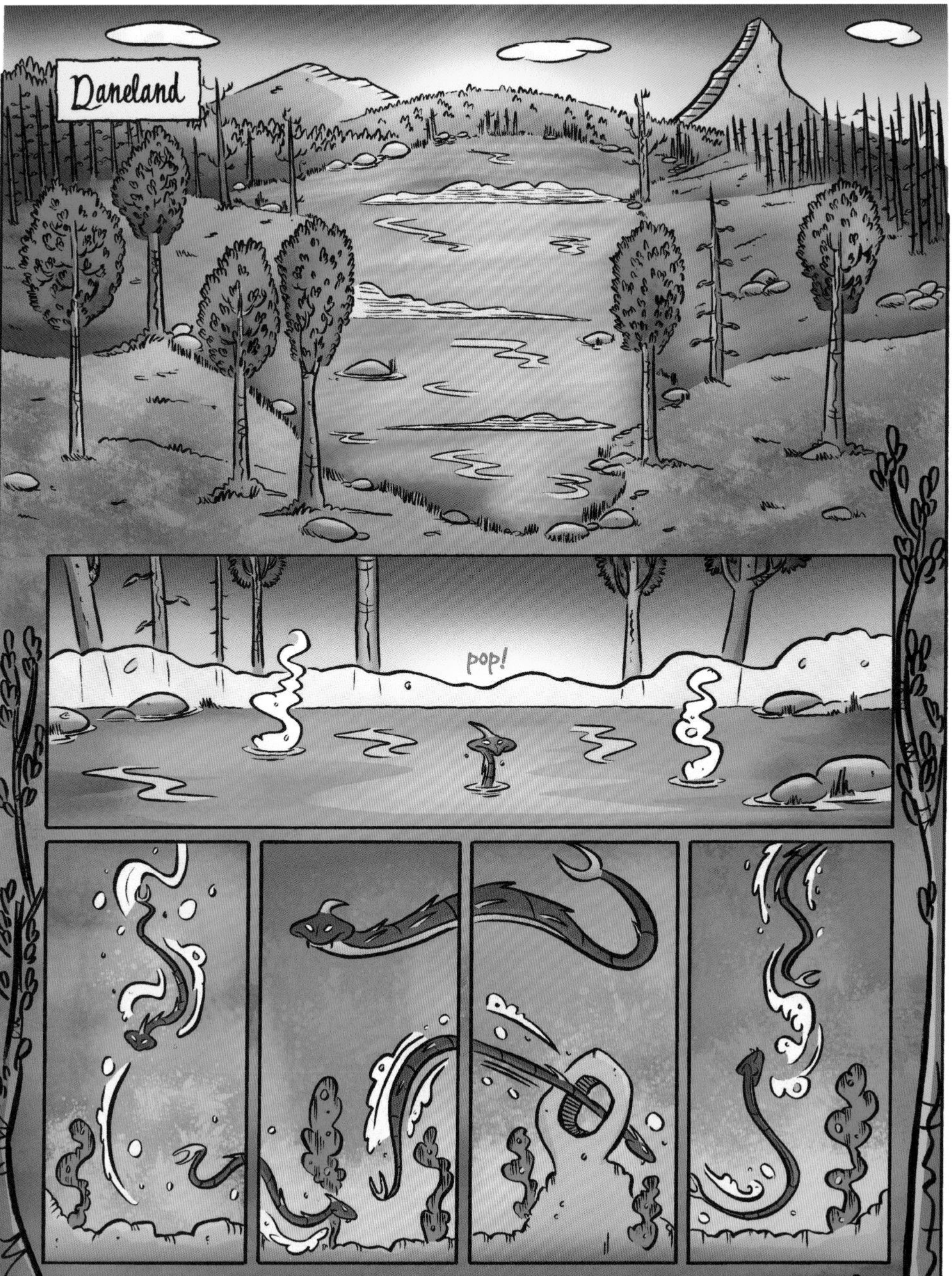
Daneland
pop!

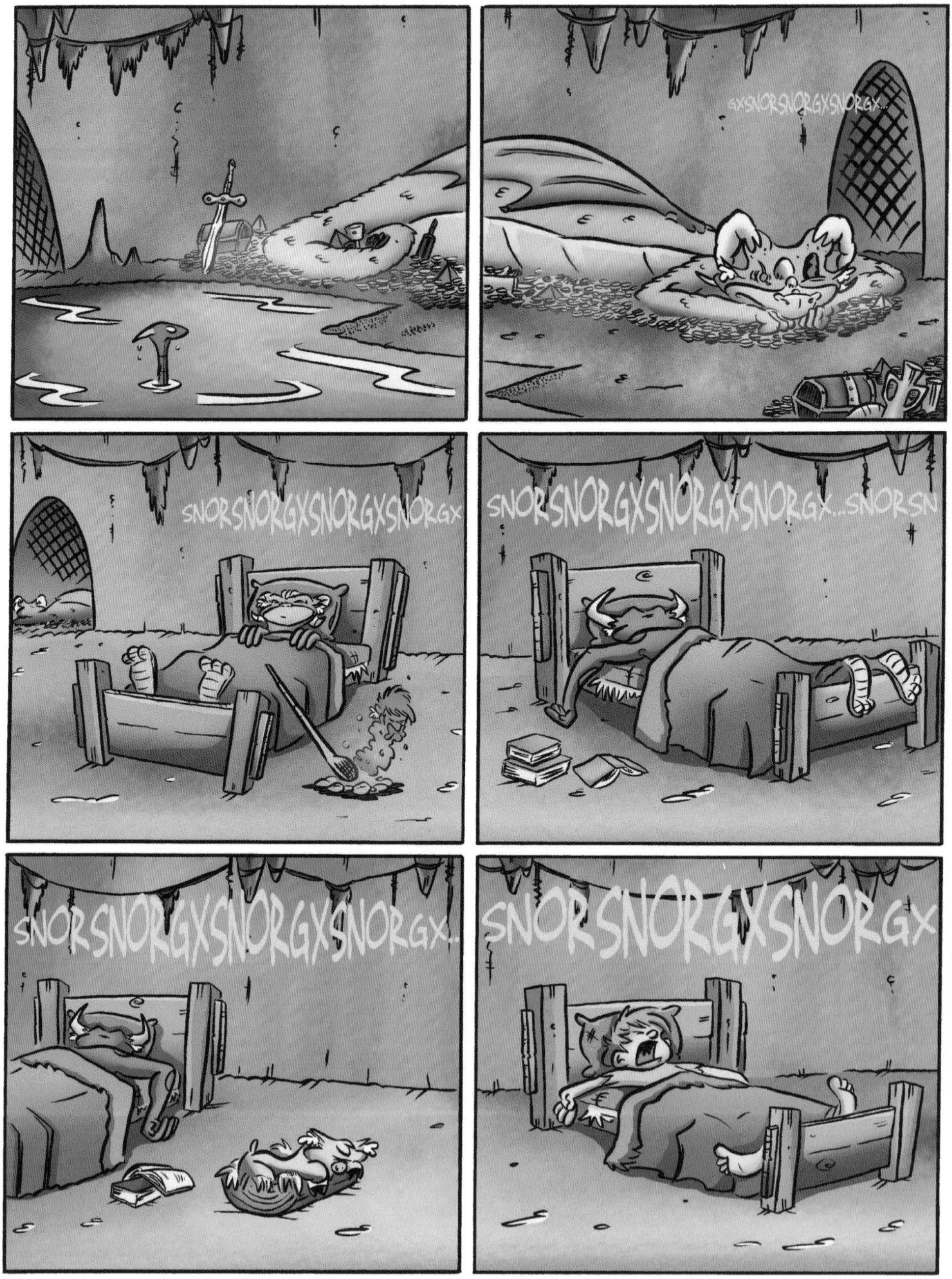
GXSNORSNORGXSNORGX...
SNORSNORGXSNORGXSNORGX
SNORSNORGXSNORGXSNORGX...SNORSN
SNORSNORGXSNORGXSNORGX..
SNORSNORGXSNORGX

Lookin' for Lingonberries

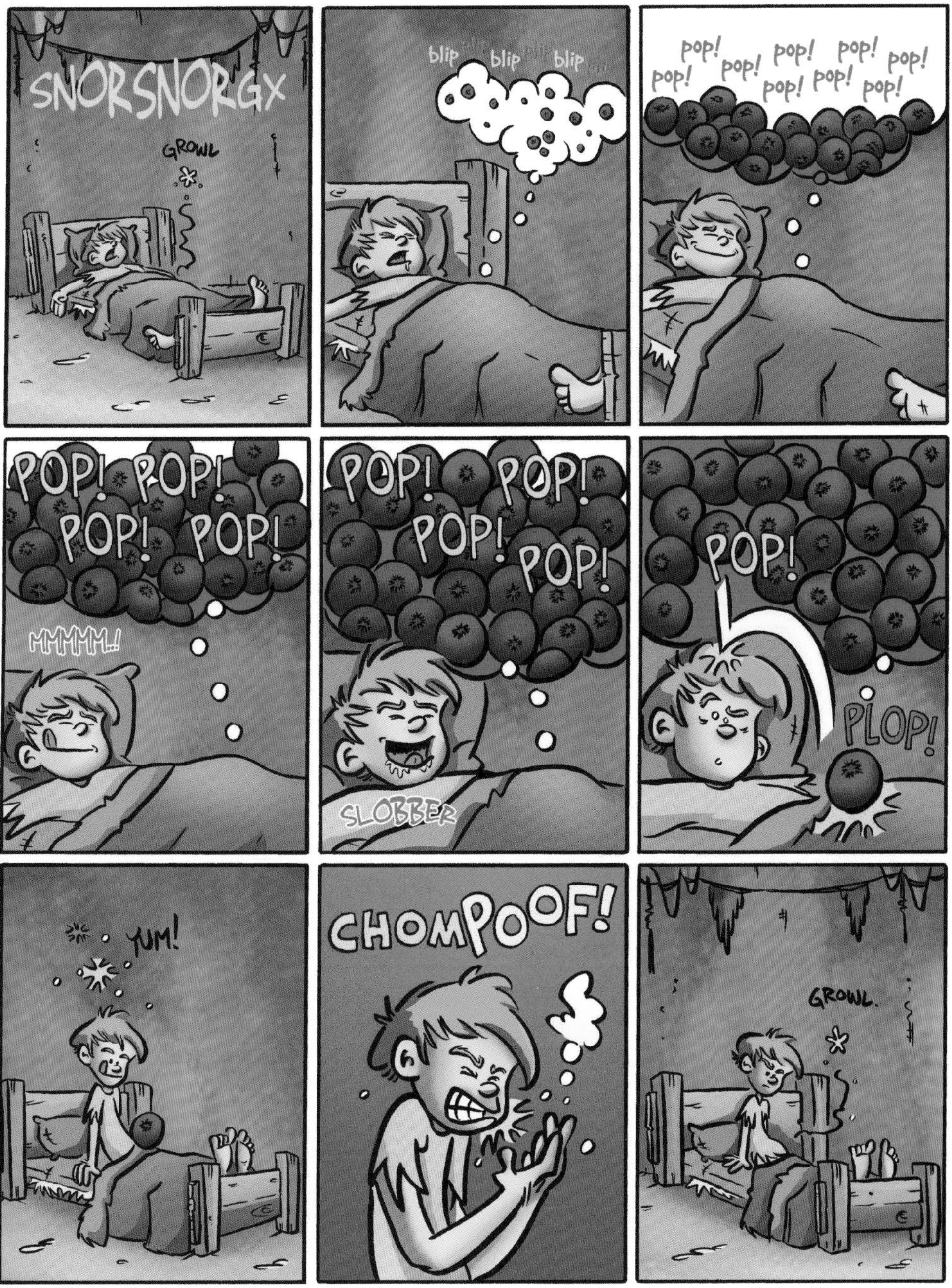

SNORSNORGX
GROWL
blip blip blip
pop! pop! pop! pop! pop! pop! pop! pop! pop!
POP! POP! POP! POP!
MMMMM..!
POP! POP! POP! POP!
SLOBBER
POP!
PLOP!
YUM!
CHOMPOOF!
GROWL.

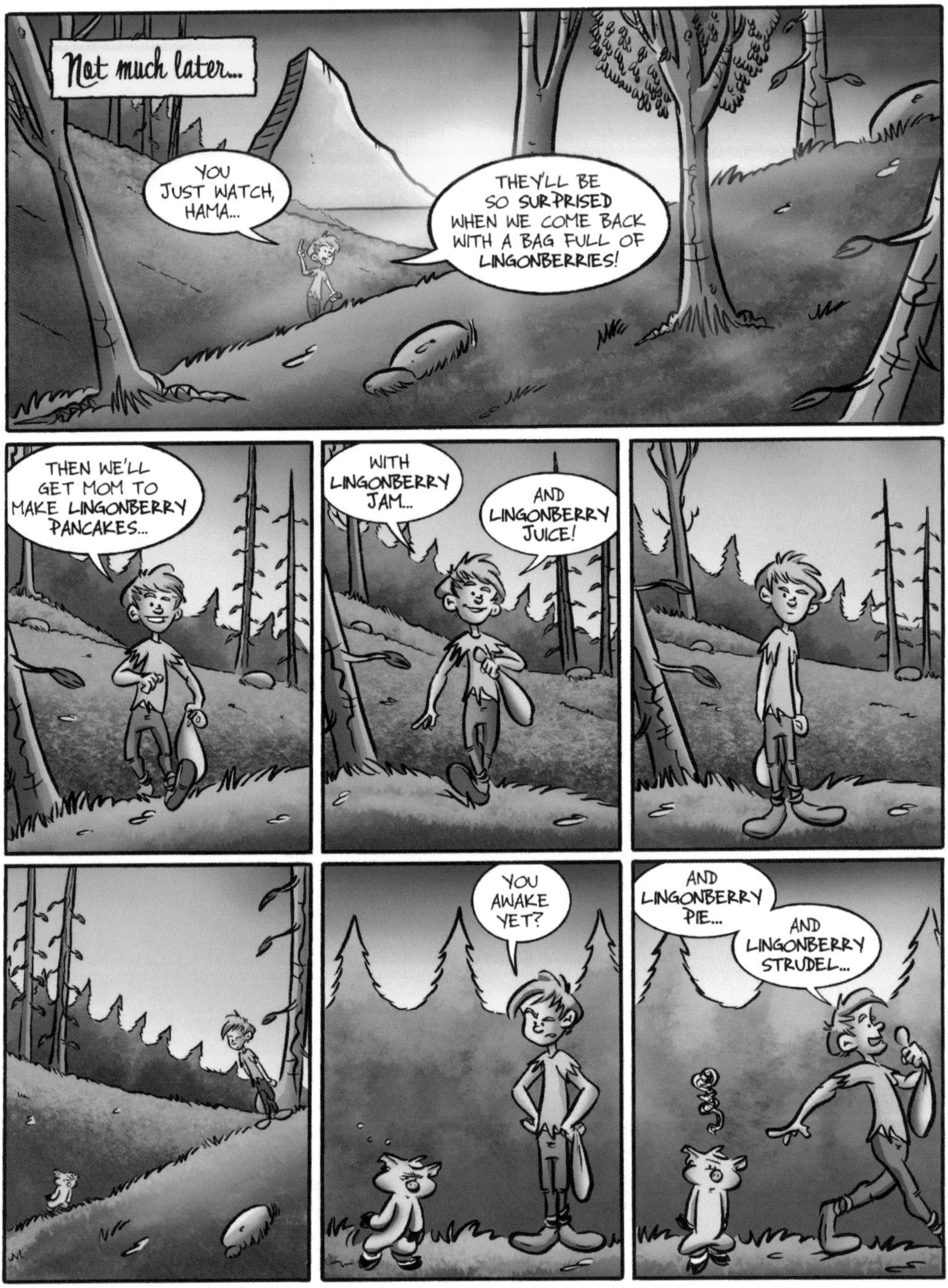
Not much later...
YOU JUST WATCH, HAMA...
THEY'LL BE SO SURPRISED WHEN WE COME BACK WITH A BAG FULL OF LINGONBERRIES!
THEN WE'LL GET MOM TO MAKE LINGONBERRY PANCAKES...
WITH LINGONBERRY JAM...
AND LINGONBERRY JUICE!
YOU AWAKE YET?
AND LINGONBERRY PIE...
AND LINGONBERRY STRUDEL...

Lookin' for Lingonberries

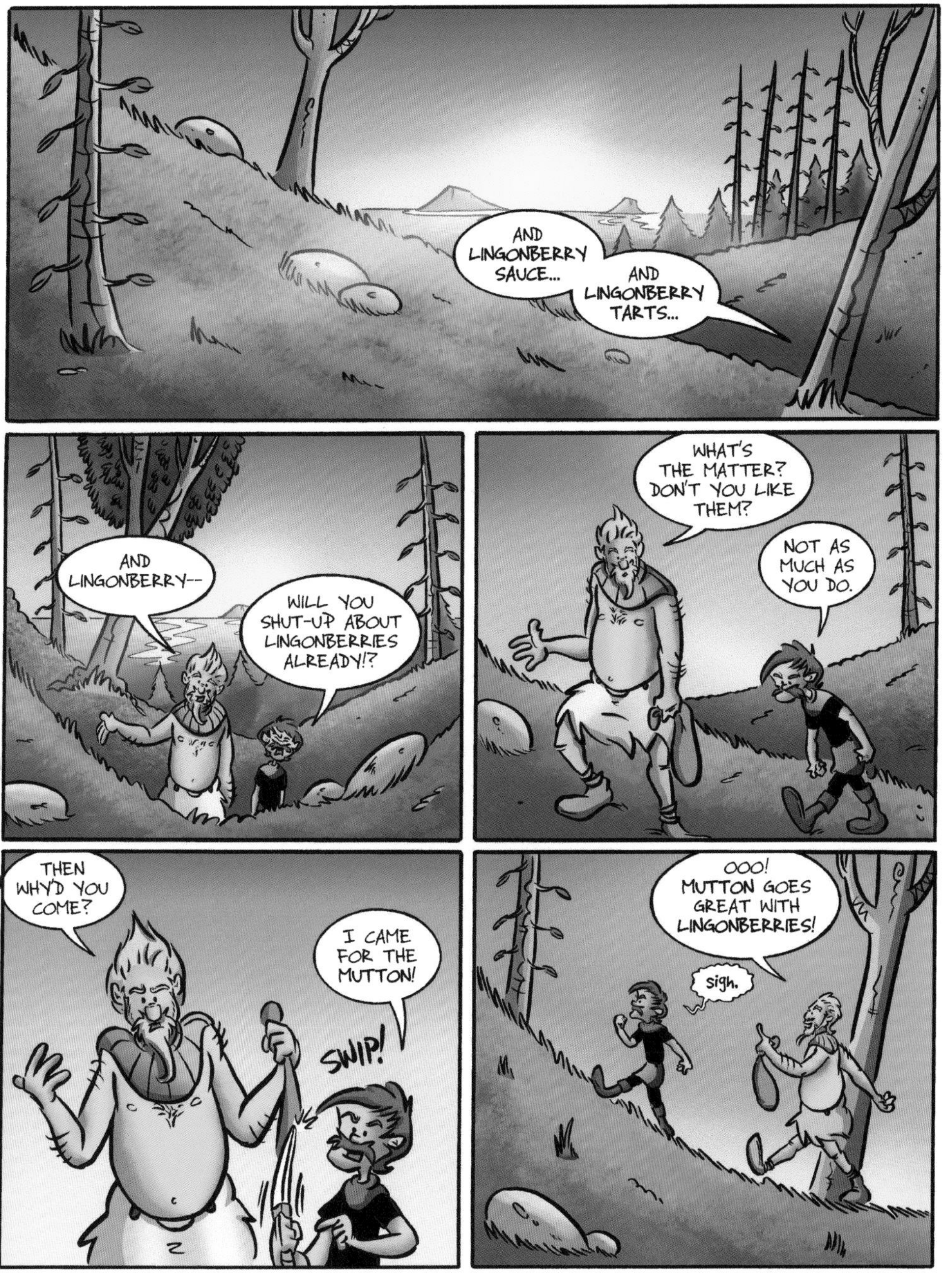

AND LINGONBERRY SAUCE...
AND LINGONBERRY TARTS...
AND LINGONBERRY--
WILL YOU SHUT-UP ABOUT LINGONBERRIES ALREADY!?
WHAT'S THE MATTER? DON'T YOU LIKE THEM?
NOT AS MUCH AS YOU DO.
THEN WHY'D YOU COME?
I CAME FOR THE MUTTON!
SWIP!
OOO! MUTTON GOES GREAT WITH LINGONBERRIES!
sigh.

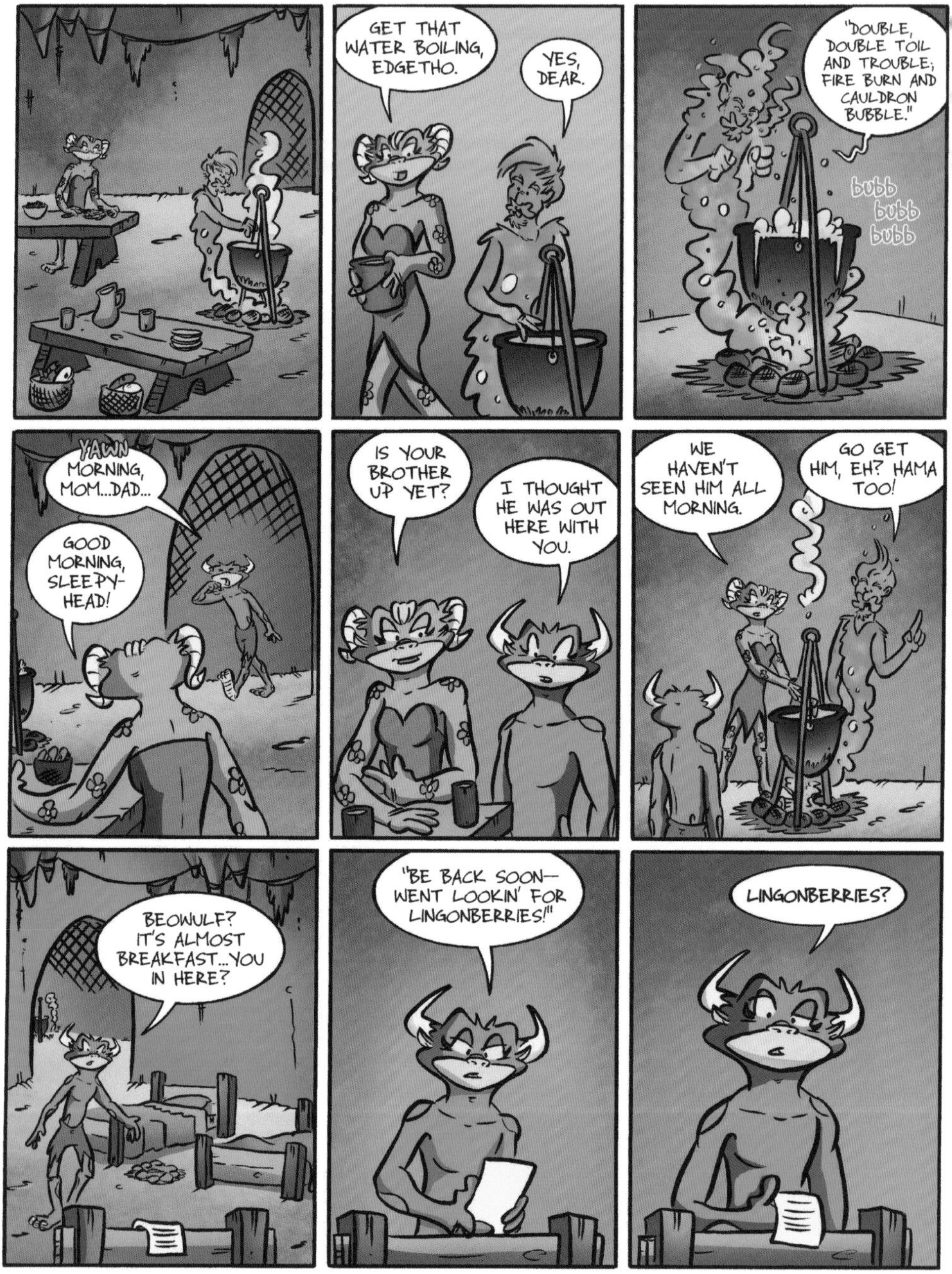
GET THAT WATER BOILING, EDGETHO.
YES, DEAR.
"DOUBLE, DOUBLE TOIL AND TROUBLE; FIRE BURN AND CAULDRON BUBBLE."
bubb bubb bubb
YAWN
MORNING, MOM...DAD...
GOOD MORNING, SLEEPY-HEAD!
IS YOUR BROTHER UP YET?
I THOUGHT HE WAS OUT HERE WITH YOU.
WE HAVEN'T SEEN HIM ALL MORNING.
GO GET HIM, EH? HAMA TOO!
BEOWULF? IT'S ALMOST BREAKFAST...YOU IN HERE?
"BE BACK SOON— WENT LOOKIN' FOR LINGONBERRIES!"
LINGONBERRIES?

LOOKIN' FOR LINGONBERRIES

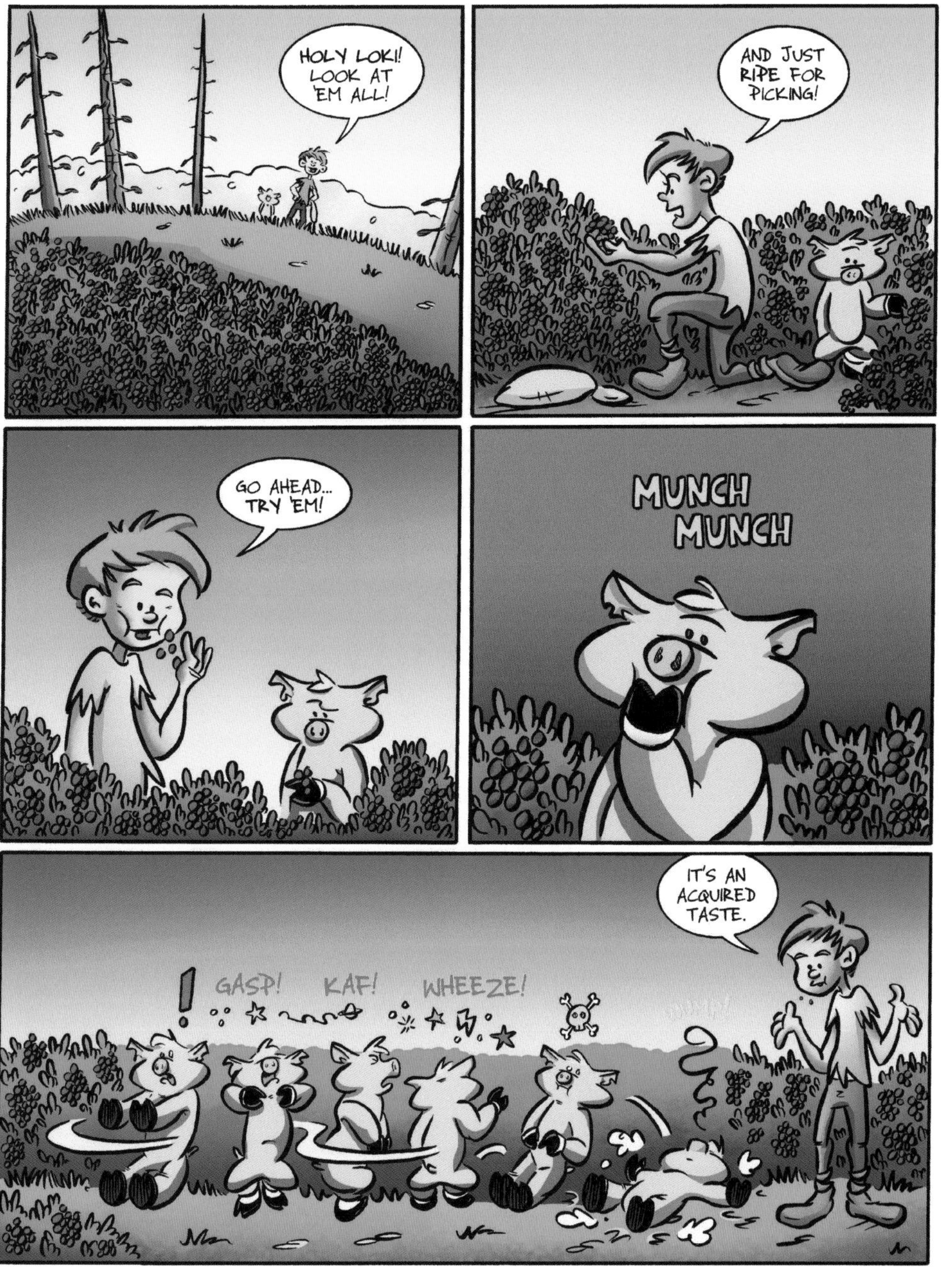
HOLY LOKI! LOOK AT 'EM ALL!
AND JUST RIPE FOR PICKING!
GO AHEAD... TRY 'EM!
MUNCH MUNCH
IT'S AN ACQUIRED TASTE.
!
GASP!
KAF!
WHEEZE!

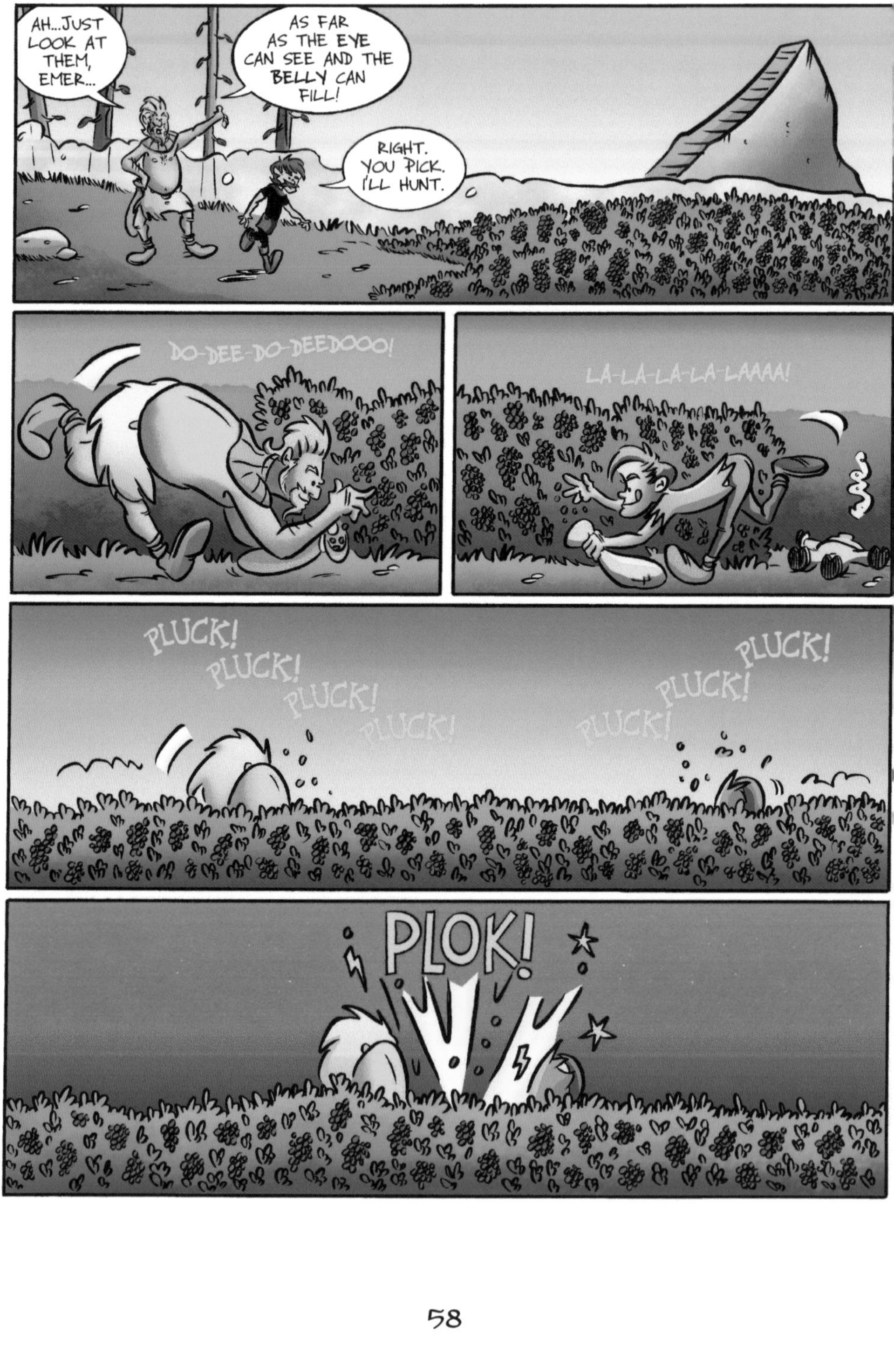
AH...JUST LOOK AT THEM, EMER...
AS FAR AS THE EYE CAN SEE AND THE BELLY CAN FILL!
RIGHT. YOU PICK. I'LL HUNT.
DO-DEE-DO-DEEDOOO!
LA-LA-LA-LA-LAAAA!
PLUCK! PLUCK! PLUCK! PLUCK!
PLUCK! PLUCK! PLUCK!
PLOK!

Lookin' for Lingonberries

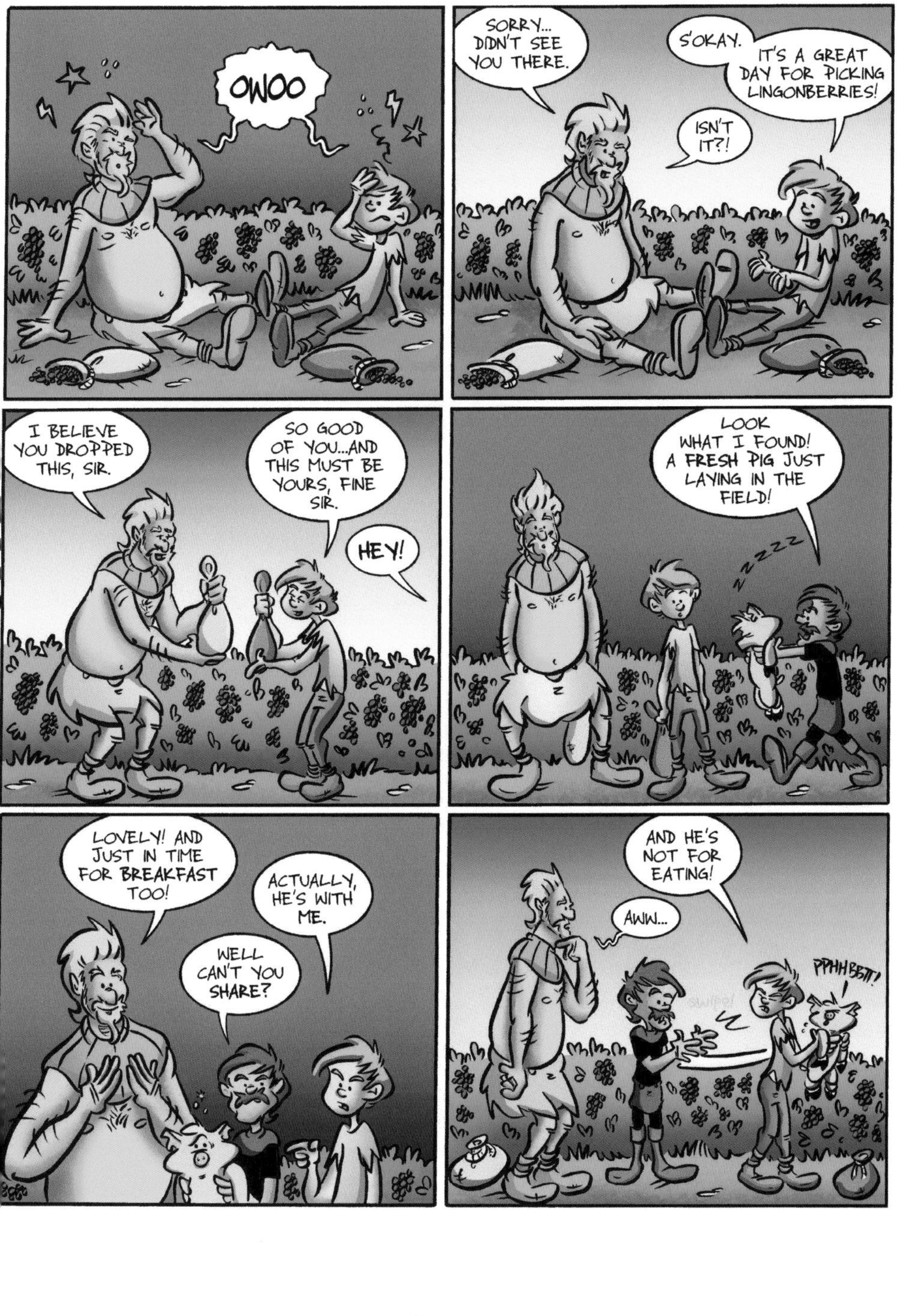
OWOO
SORRY... DIDN'T SEE YOU THERE.
S'OKAY.
IT'S A GREAT DAY FOR PICKING LINGONBERRIES!
ISN'T IT?!
I BELIEVE YOU DROPPED THIS, SIR.
SO GOOD OF YOU...AND THIS MUST BE YOURS, FINE SIR.
HEY!
LOOK WHAT I FOUND! A FRESH PIG JUST LAYING IN THE FIELD!
ZZZZZ
LOVELY! AND JUST IN TIME FOR BREAKFAST TOO!
ACTUALLY, HE'S WITH ME.
WELL CAN'T YOU SHARE?
AND HE'S NOT FOR EATING!
AWW...
PPHHBBT!

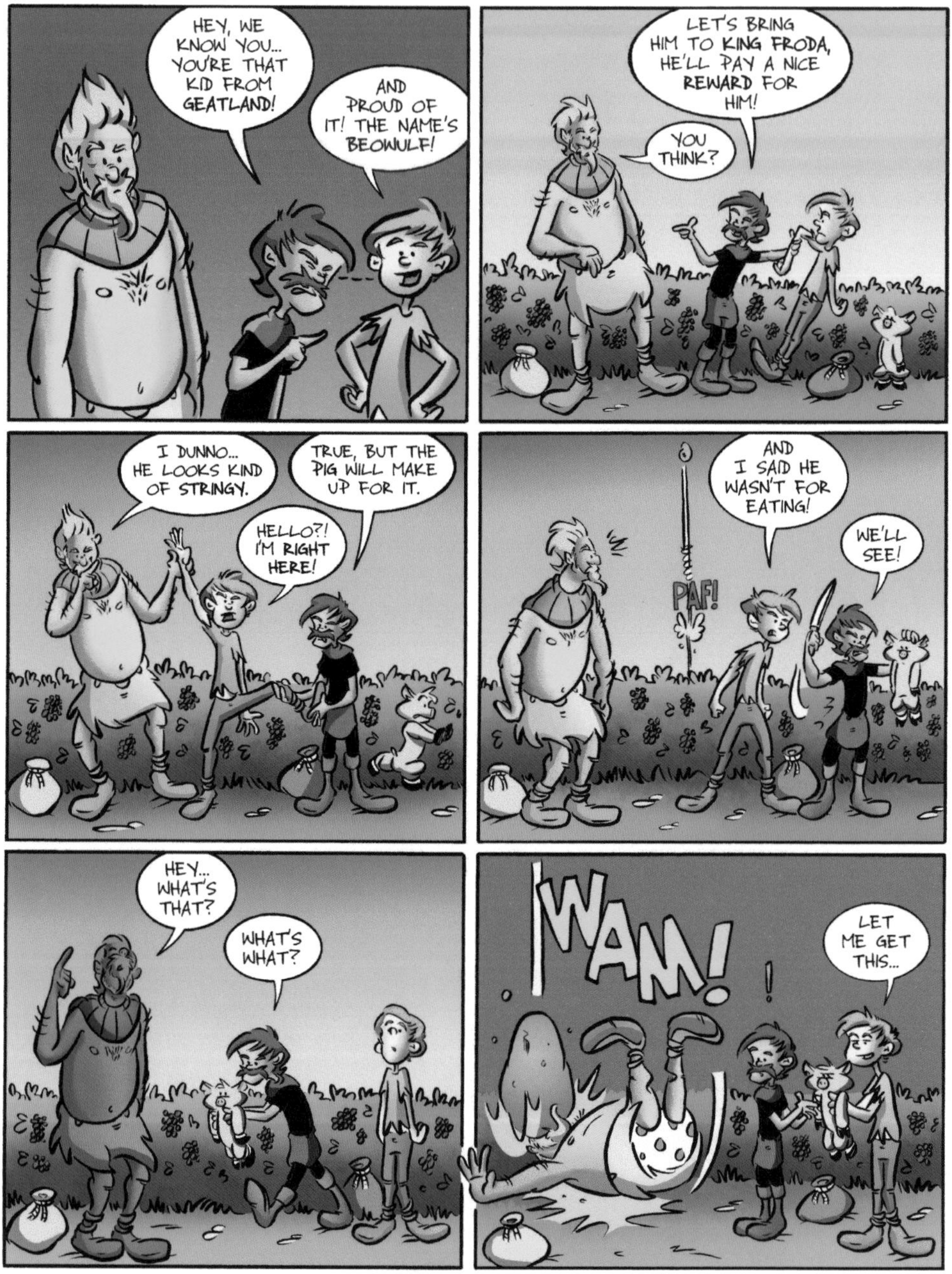
HEY, WE KNOW YOU... YOU'RE THAT KID FROM GEATLAND!
AND PROUD OF IT! THE NAME'S BEOWULF!
LET'S BRING HIM TO KING FRODA, HE'LL PAY A NICE REWARD FOR HIM!
YOU THINK?
I DUNNO... HE LOOKS KIND OF STRINGY.
TRUE, BUT THE PIG WILL MAKE UP FOR IT.
HELLO?! I'M RIGHT HERE!
PAF!
AND I SAID HE WASN'T FOR EATING!
WE'LL SEE!
HEY... WHAT'S THAT?
WHAT'S WHAT?
WAM!
LET ME GET THIS...

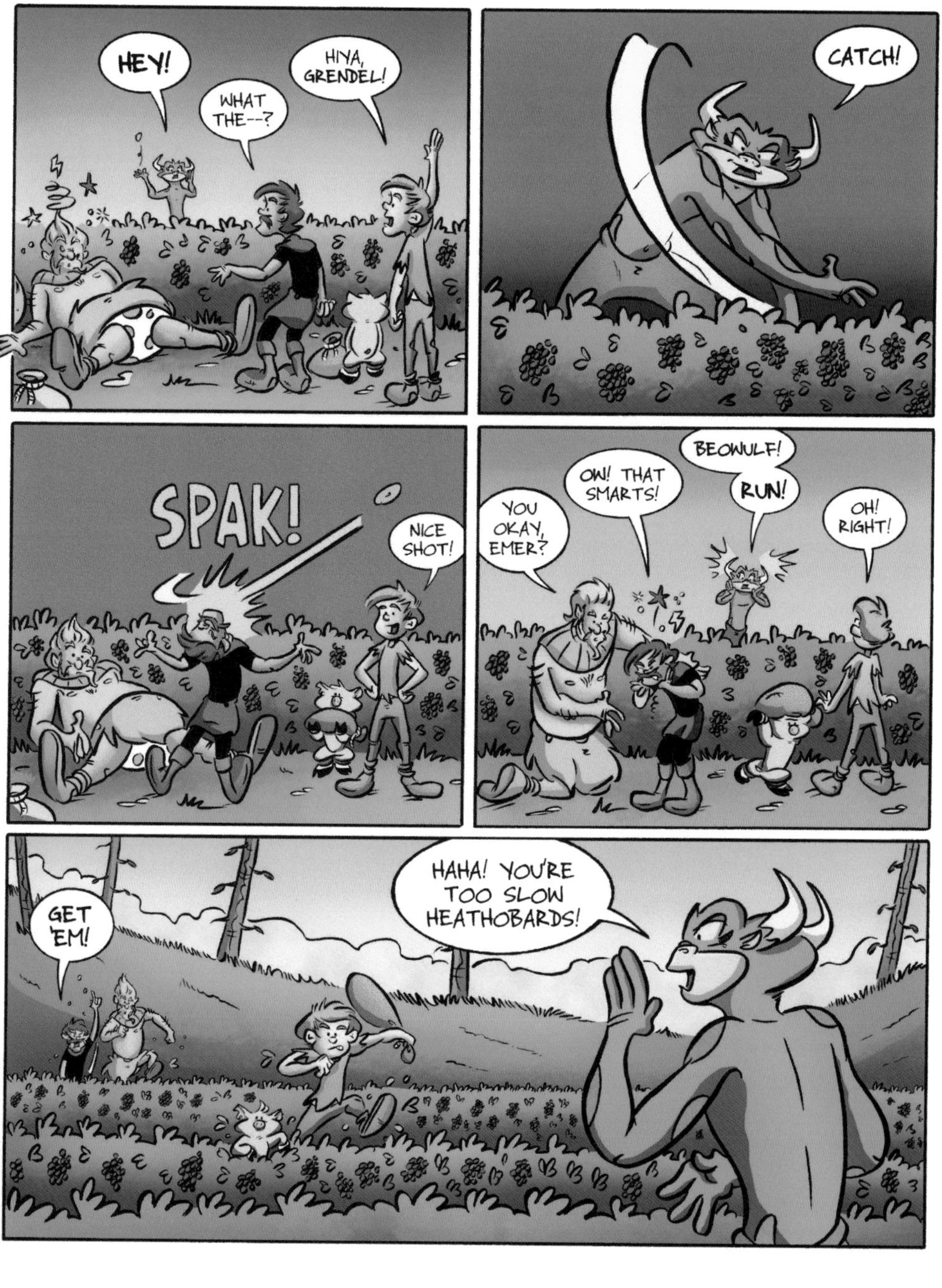
HEY!
WHAT THE--?
HIYA, GRENDEL!
CATCH!
SPAK!
NICE SHOT!
YOU OKAY, EMER?
OW! THAT SMARTS!
BEOWULF! RUN!
OH! RIGHT!
GET 'EM!
HAHA! YOU'RE TOO SLOW HEATHOBARDS!

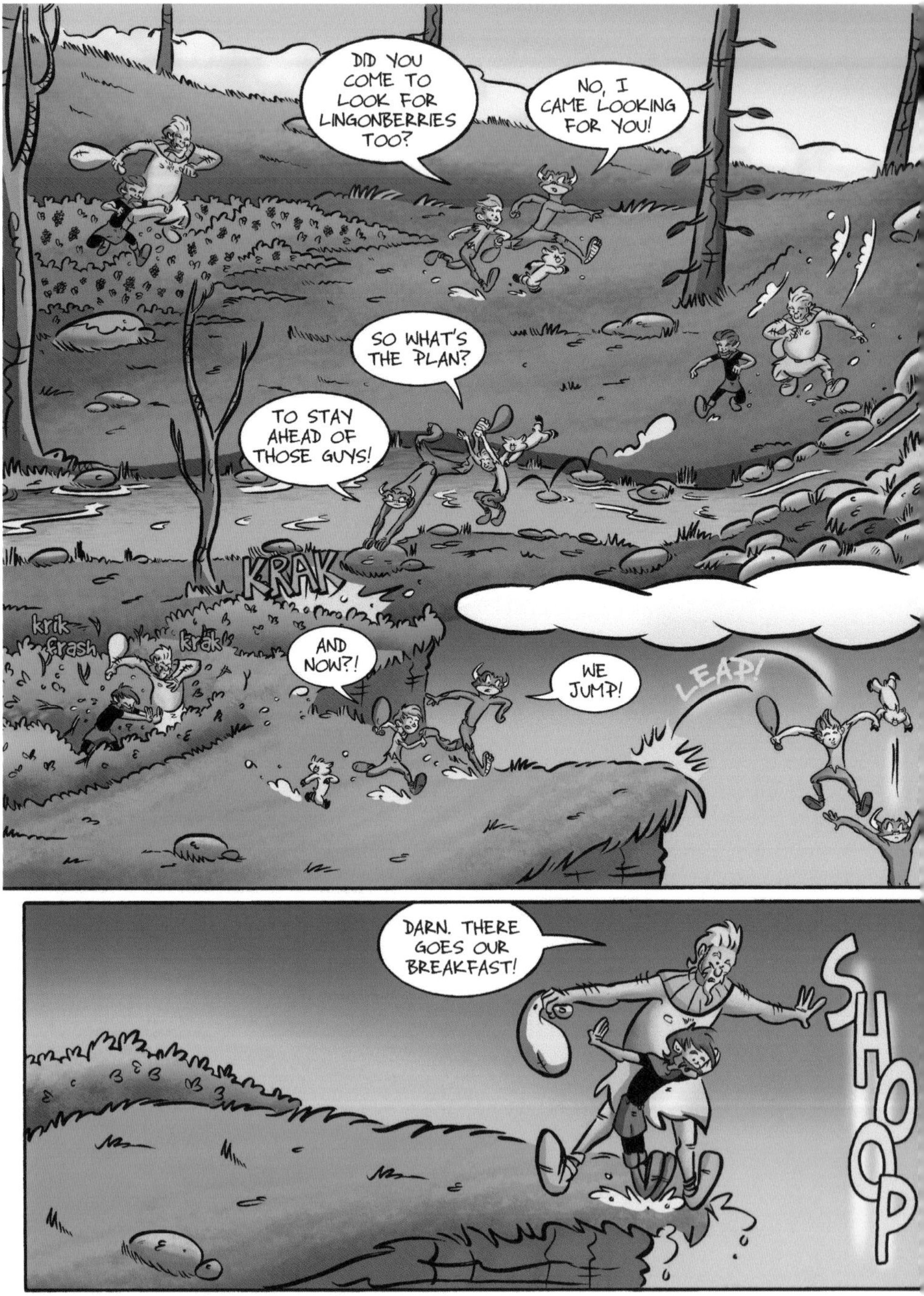
DID YOU COME TO LOOK FOR LINGONBERRIES TOO?
NO, I CAME LOOKING FOR YOU!
SO WHAT'S THE PLAN?
TO STAY AHEAD OF THOSE GUYS!
KRAK
krik
frash
krak
AND NOW?!
WE JUMP!
LEAP!
DARN. THERE GOES OUR BREAKFAST!
SHOOP

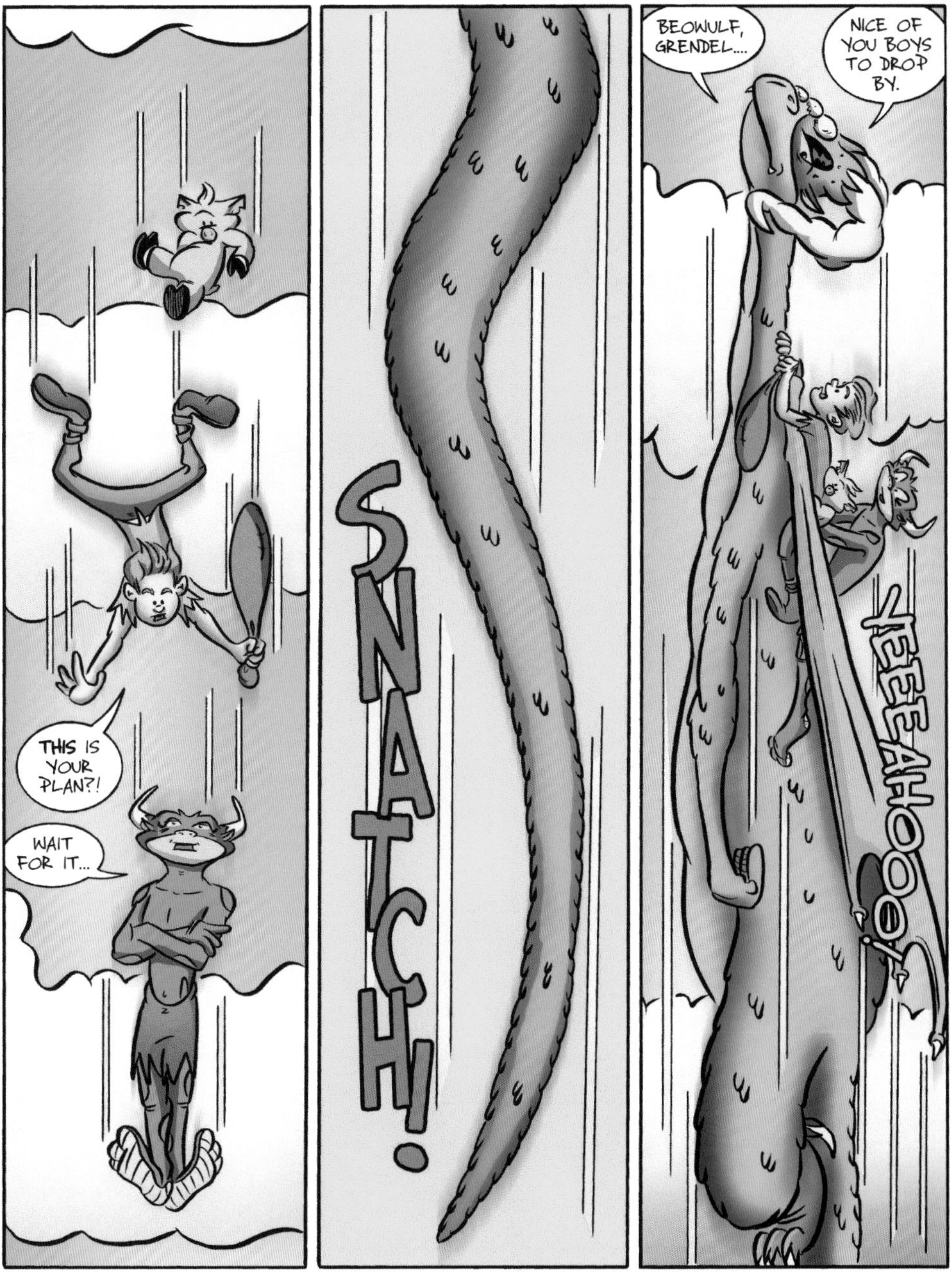
THIS IS YOUR PLAN?!
WAIT FOR IT...
SNATCH!
BEOWULF, GRENDEL....
NICE OF YOU BOYS TO DROP BY.
YEEEAHOOO!

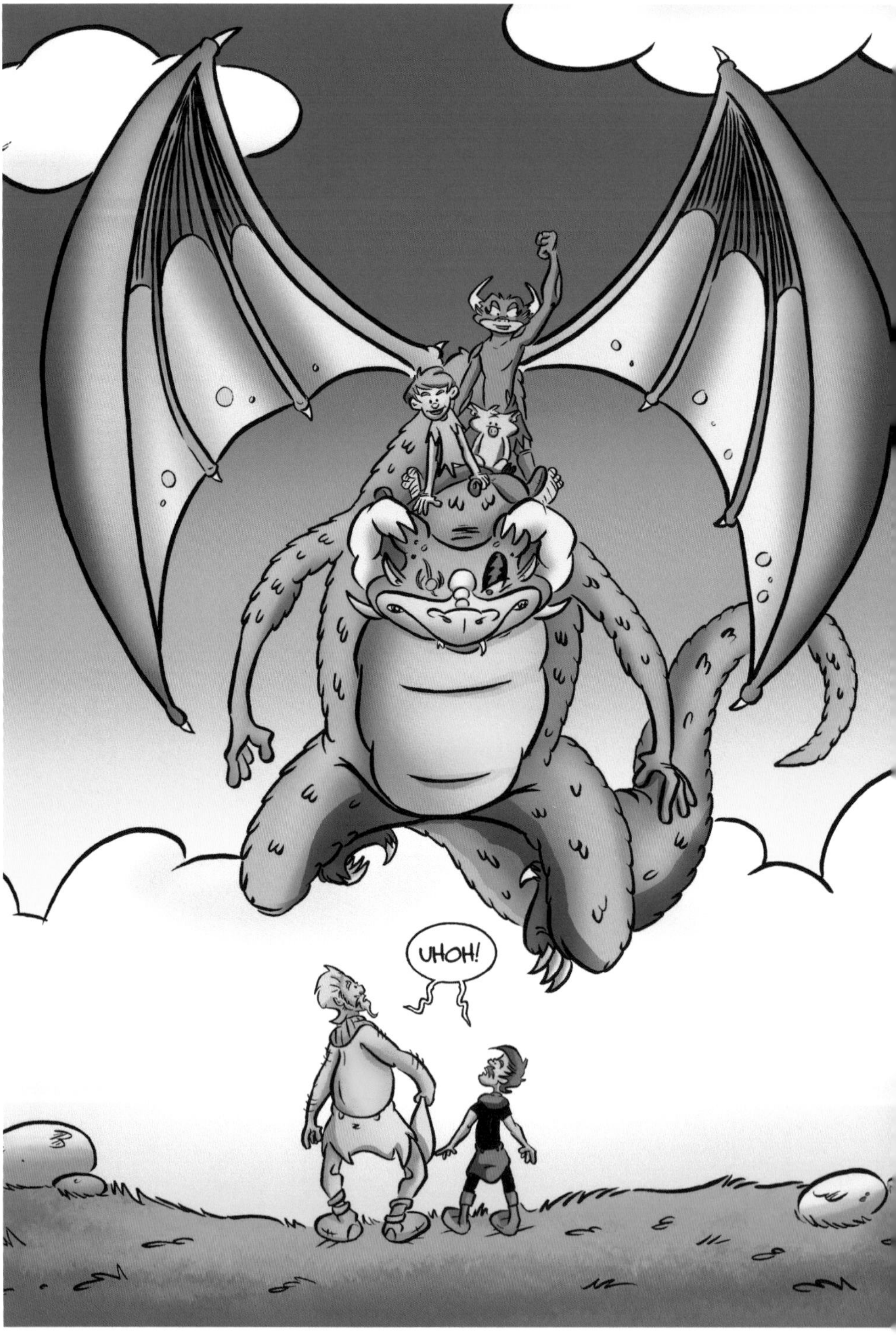
UHOH!

Lookin' for Lingonberries

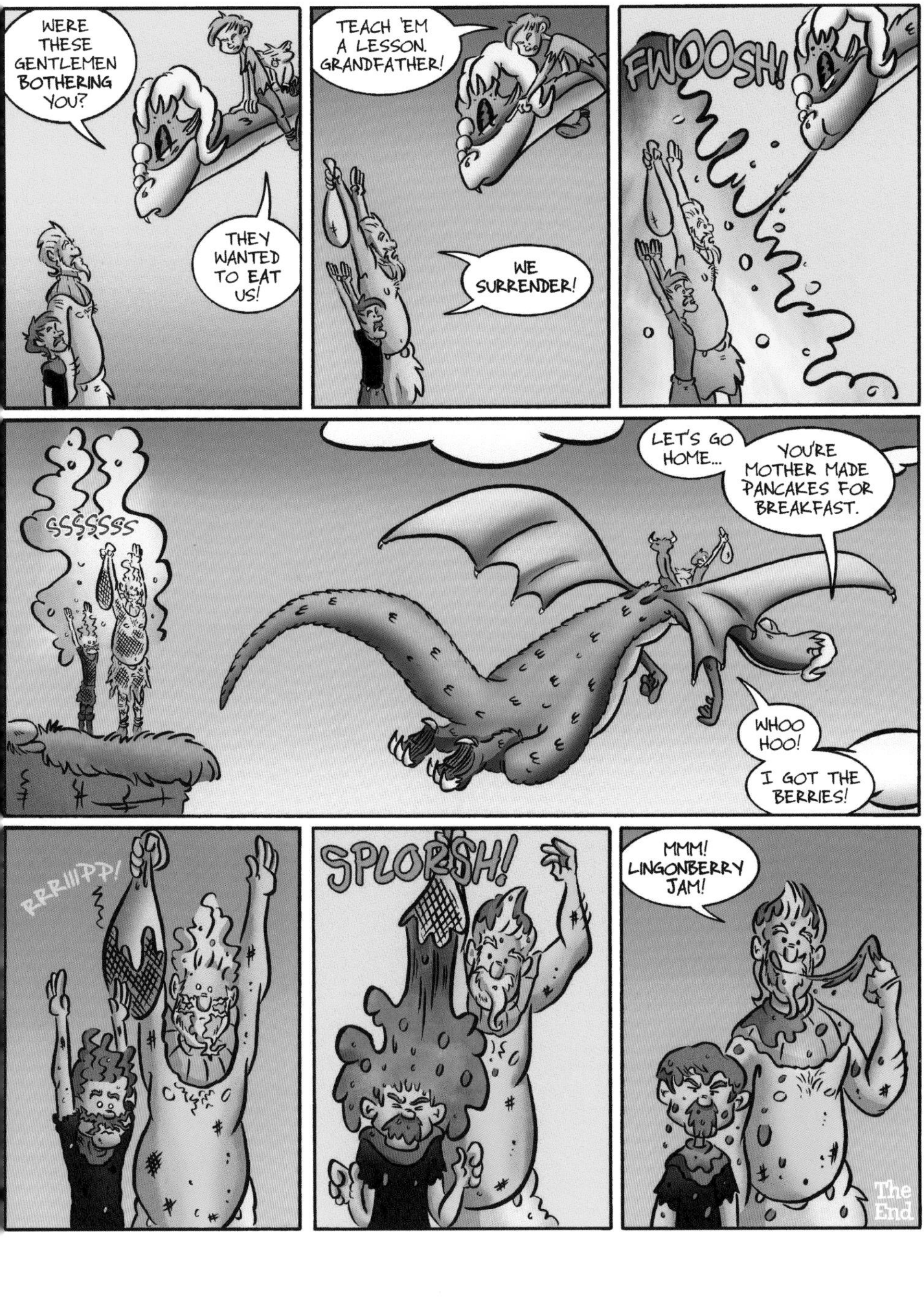

WERE THESE GENTLEMEN BOTHERING YOU?
THEY WANTED TO EAT US!
TEACH 'EM A LESSON. GRANDFATHER!
WE SURRENDER!
FWOOSH!
SSSSSSS
LET'S GO HOME...
YOU'RE MOTHER MADE PANCAKES FOR BREAKFAST.
WHOO HOO!
I GOT THE BERRIES!
RRRIIIPP!
SPLORSH!
MMM! LINGONBERRY JAM!
The End

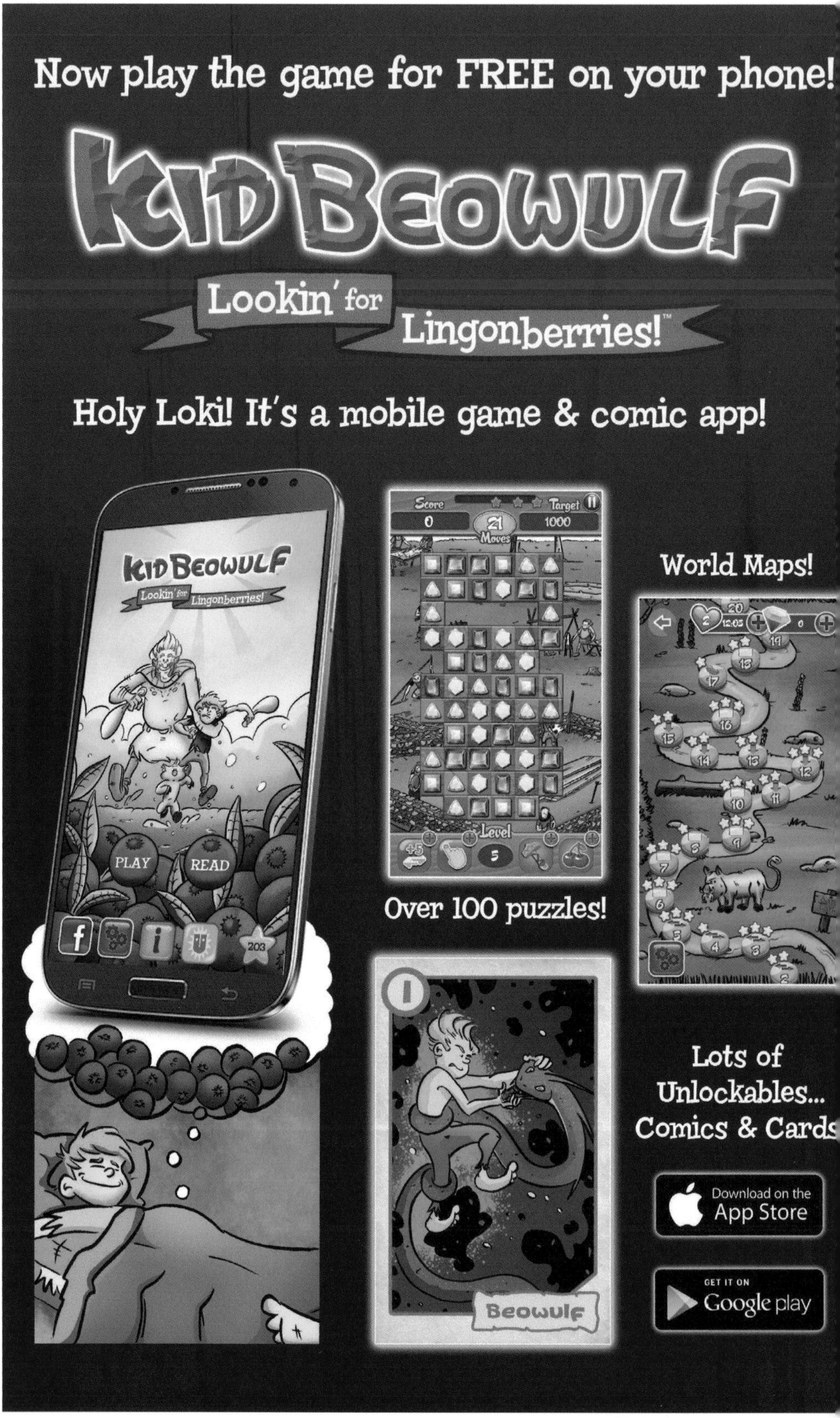

Now play the game for FREE on your phone!
KID BEOWULF
Lookin' for Lingonberries!™
Holy Loki! It's a mobile game & comic app!
PLAY
READ
Score
Target
0
21
Moves
1000
Level
5
Over 100 puzzles!
World Maps!
Beowulf
Lots of Unlockables... Comics & Cards
Download on the App Store
GET IT ON Google play

Two brothers, a pig, and a talking sword.

1
Fajardo
Kid Beowulf the Blood-Bound Oath
Kid Beowulf
the Blood-Bound Oath
Alexis E. Fajardo

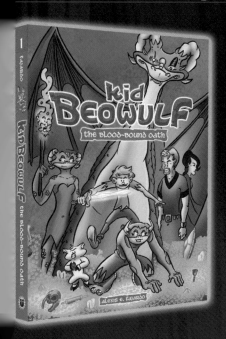

The adventures of twin brothers Beowulf and Grendel begin here!

Kid Beowulf: The Blood-Bound Oath **is book one in the *Kid Beowulf* series and explores the mysterious origins of twin brothers Beowulf and Grendel, their monstrous (but loving) mother, Gertrude, and their fire-breathing one-eyed grandfather, the Dragon!**

Filled with action, adventure, and mythology, this is a great book for fans of *Bone* and *Amulet*!

"What Rick Riordan did for the Greek gods, Fajardo has done for *Beowulf*: magnificent." – Kirkus Review

The adventure continues in book two!

Kid Beowulf: The Song Of Roland **s the second book in the series and llows Beowulf and Grendel on their adventure in France!**

In search of their lost uncle, the rothers find a kingdom in shambles: ng Charlemagne is ailing, his knights have been exiled and France's hero Roland needs a kick in the pants! Can Beowulf and Grendel unite the ingdom before it's taken over by an invading Saracen horde?

2
Fajardo
Kid Beowulf the Song of Roland
Kid Beowulf
the Song of Roland
Alexis E. Fajardo

amp! COMICS for kids

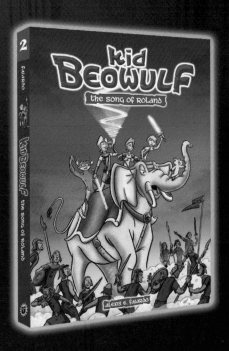

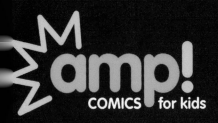

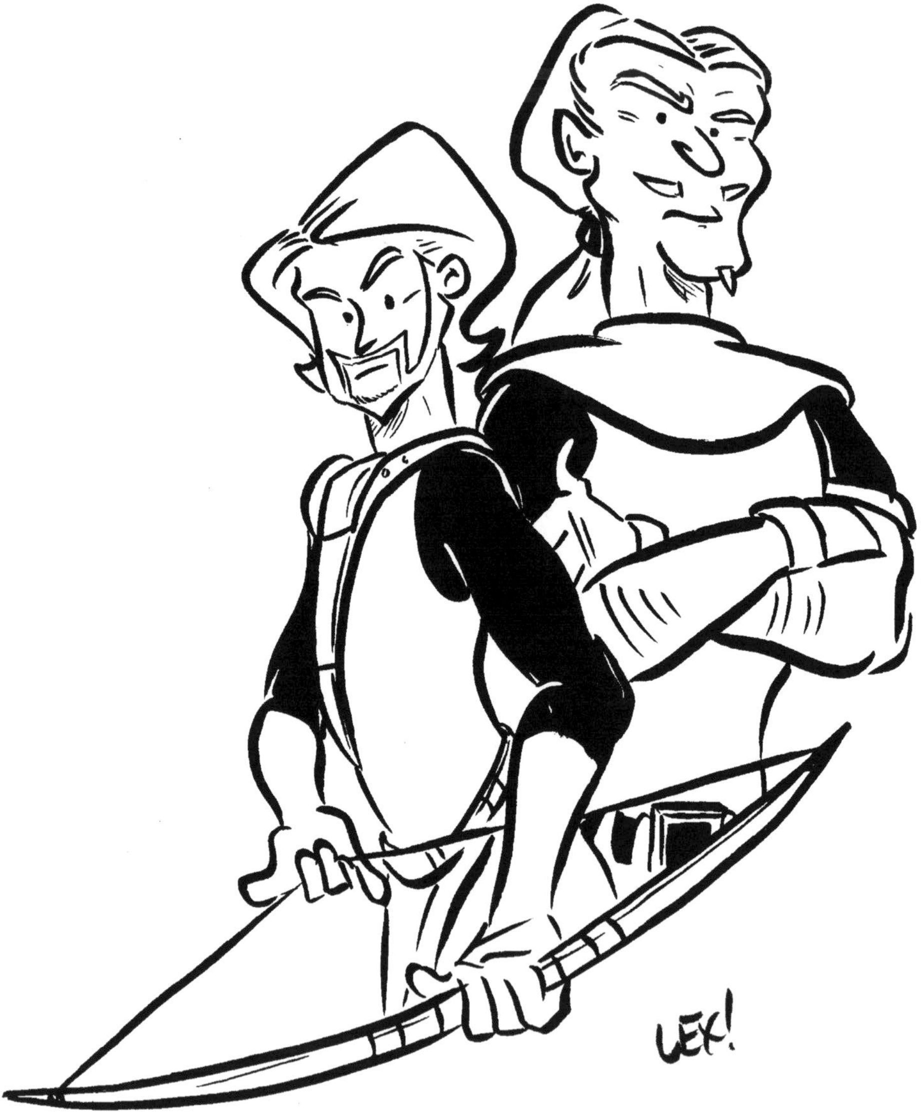
LEX!

Visit the official Kid Beowulf website at kidbeowulf.com
Follow Lex on Twitter & Instagram @LexKidB
Become a fan on Facebook at www.facebook.com/kidbeowulf

CPSIA information can be obtained at www.ICGtesting.com
Printed in the USA
LVIW01n1611061217
558855LV00008B/105